By Antonio Escohotado

Reality and Substance (1986)

Philosophy and Methodology in the Sciences (1987)

The Spirit of Comedy (1991)

Whores and Wives (1993)

From Physis to Polis (1995)

The Question of Cannabis (1997)

Portrait of a Libertine (1998)

Chaos and Order (2000)

Learning About Drugs (2002)

Sixty Weeks in the Tropics (2003)

Elementary History of Drugs (2003)

Four Myths on Sex and Duty (2003)

The Enemies of Commerce (2008)

THE
GENERAL HISTORY
OF
DRUGS

Volume Two Part Two

Antonio Escohotado

translated and edited by
G. W. Robinette

GRAFFITI MILITANTE PRESS
Valparaiso, Chile
2021

Front Cover: *The Witches' Kitchen* (ca. 1610), Frans Francken the Younger (1581 – 1642), Kunsthistorisches Museum, Vienna.

For Albert Hofmann and Tom Szasz, who with their friendship and advice helped to distill the essence of this chronicle.

This endeavor to achieve that everyone should approve that which one loves and hates is, in reality, ambition; and thus we see that each naturally desires that the rest should live according to his own nature. But as all desire this at the same time, at once each one gets in the way of the other, and as everyone wishes to be praised and loved by everyone else, they end by hating one another.
– B. Spinoza, <u>Ethics</u> (Book III, Proposition XXXI)

I owe gratitude also to Pablo Fernandez-Florez, who was always distrustful of the project even though he ended up writing various portions and who contributed valuable documentation for the rest; to Luis Gil, who guided me decisively through Greco-Latin antiquity, moreover remediating some inappropriate remarks in the proofs; to Ramon Sala, for making accessible to me many sources about the contemporary period; and to Monica Bacazar, my wife, who stoically supported the birth of the whole book, collaborating also in the typewritten transcription. With their economic assistence, the Center for Sociological Investigations first, and later the Ministry of Culture, permitted an undivided attention to the work in its initial and final stages.

THE GENERAL HISTORY OF DRUGS VOLUME 2 PART 2

Author's Preface
to Volume One

It has not been very common to unite theory and practice in the matter of drugs, and this explains perhaps some adventures that accompanied the composition of _La historia general de las drogas_. In 1988 – being then a professor of Sociology – the criminal court of Palma condemned me to two years and a day of prison, having found me guilty of drug trafficking. The punishment requested by the prosecutor – six years – was reduced by two-thirds, because for one judge of the court the offence was found to be _en grado de tentativa imposible_ [literally, a crime impossible to commit]. Effectively, those who were offering to sell and those who were offering to buy – by means of three interposed users (one of whom was myself) – were agents of the police or their pawns. Just one week after this judgment, the criminal court of Cordoba declared a verdict of pure entrapment upon similar facts, whereupon they proceeded to annul all the charges, an interpretation that in time would become the accepted jurisprudence in Spain.

Apprehensive over what might end up happening on an appeal to the Supreme Court – in a litigation where a certain citizen was alleging to have been blackmailed by the authorities, while they were accusing him of being an opulent drug dealer who hid his criminal empire behind the lectern of the scholar – I preferred to serve the sentence without delay. As a then magistrate of the Supreme Court made clear, the matter was poisoned by the fact of my being a spokesperson for reform on the issue, already well-known since 1983. Given the facts of the case, to absolve without conditions would incriminate in some manner the incriminator, and would open a path toward a demand for a scandalous reparation.

After some inquiries, I discovered that the jail at Cuenca – thanks to its understanding Director – would concede me the three things necessary to take advantage of such a stay: a light switch inside the cell, an ancient PC, and isolation. During that fully-paid (albeit humble) vacation, four-fifths of this work was written. Naturally, I had entered into that establishment with no small number of kilos of index cards and notes, gathered during many long years. I had only to structure them, polishing the final exposition.

It could be added that I did not lose much time, and for this same reason neither was I downhearted. However, the conditions for bibliographic consultation are not ideal in a penitentiary and before I could abandon it this book began to be published,[1] so that it was dogged from the beginning by innumerable imprecisions, more than those which trouble any really extensive work. Some of them were remediated in the third edition, thanks above all to the effort of the chemist and ethnobotanist Jonathan Ott who tirelessly inserted the many changes and additions necessary, thoroughly revising the system of references and transforming entire sections of the text.

With this new English edition, the degree of precision demanded in a scientific work has been perfected once more, completed by a researcher who has been able to confirm and amplify my work making use of various libraries and the internet. As a result, the edition that the reader now holds in his hands not only suffers from far fewer errors and oversights, but also hopes to fulfill even closer the goal of an academic standard with regards to the precision of its information. No doubt, in twenty years this history will need to be revised again as new data becomes available. I look forward to reading that book.

La Navata
February 2010

---

[1] Volumes I and II in the *Alianza* edition.

Translator's Preface
Volume Two Part Two

The first part of the second volume, subtitled Volume Two, Part One, was published in 2018. This is the second part of the second volume, subtitled Volume Two, Part Two. I have issued these separately due to time constraints.

During these plague years, the prohibition continues to fail. More states in the US have legalized cannabis, either recreationally or medicinally, and one (Oregon) has depenalized the personal use of practically all drugs, but we'll see. Other countries are waking up as well. The First World War on Drugs continues to collapse due to its own internal economic contradictions. One can compare in this volume the inital demonization and then reluctant relegalization of coffee, tobacco, coca, opium, *maté* and various recreational and medicinal remedies used by the witches only after long, relentless and ferocious wars that not only failed but bankrupted their respective countries and kingdoms. At which point the powers that were finally bowed to the inevitable, relicensing, retaxing and reregulating what were until so very recently for them new forms of shame if not the tools of the devil. If political self-righteousness is the root of all evil, then the lack of money is the spur to trading in and taxing sin.

Why spend the time to translate a book like Antonio's with its careful insight, attention to detail and reasoned judgment? Though a great ignorant darkness pervades the earth today, I am betting on an improbable future. History teaches us only that almost nobody ever learns from the past. But no one ever will learn without a past to reflect upon, a good and faithful rendition of their successes and failures. So far Escohotado has written the best history of drugs that exists.

I implore you to read it in the original Spanish. This first English edition of the second half of the second volume has been annotated with many primary sources newly accessible online. These help illustrate the original themes with a deeper and more nuanced understanding of drugs in the early Renaissance. In only a few instances it has also been updated to reflect changes in fact and perspective over the last thirty years. E. H. Carr called history a dialogue between the present and the past. To paraphrase Dr. Johnson, when new facts emerge, I change my mind. What do you do? It's been a privilege to do my part to bring Escohotado's work to an English language audience. All errors are mine. Enjoy.

G. W. R.
Spencer Hot Springs
May 2021

P. S. This one also is *for Gail.*

Contents
of
Volume Two Part Two

Illustrations
Volume Two Part Two

THE GENERAL HISTORY OF DRUGS VOLUME 2 PART 2

Introduction
Volume Two Part Two

<hr>

This part of the story covers the early Renaissance. Chapter Eleven introduces the zeitgeist of the epoch, understood as the free examination of things and their causes. This new attitude provokes an unprecedented opposition. The Counter-Reformation initiates a crusade against witchcraft as a strategy of social control. Kraemer and Sprenger publish the _Malleus Malleficarum_ (1484). A mere accusation of witchcraft is enough to result in torture, mutilation and execution. Pico della Mirandola publishes his manifesto of resistance, the _Oratio de hominis dignitate_ (1486). The possession of unguents and herbs leads to the bonfire. The inquisitors extort money from the victims and their families.

Chapter Twelve introduces Pietro Pomponazzi whose work _De Incantationibus_ suggested that natural causes were sufficient to explain so-called diabolic phenomena. Pedro de Valencia investigates the _aquelarres_ and concludes the orgiastic visions could be due to the unguents and not the Devil. The botanist Andrés de Laguna discovers the witches' stories of erotic flights are likely brought on by the plants alone. Giambattista della Porta is accused of being a magician for writing down the formula for the Fairies Oyntment. Jan de Wier thought the witches simply mad. The Portuguese herbalist Garcia da Orta demystifies opium. Paracelsus advocates heroic remedies, using the recipes of the witches in the form of pills, syrups and tinctures. Opium symbolizes modernity. New drugs appear in Europe: coffee, tea, tobacco, coca, chocolate, peyote, _poyomatli_, _ololiuhqui_ and _maté_ which are used medicinally and spiritually, then demonized, and finally either ignored or accepted.

Chapter Thirteen observes the Dutch and English take over the spice trade from the Portuguese. Opium becomes a valuable trade good. Thomas Willis cures dysentery with opium. Franz de le Boë prescribes it for snake bite. In Leiden, the physician, chemist and botanist Herman Boerhaave introduces opium to medical students from all over Europe. The English physician Thomas Sydenham uses opium to formulate his laudenum. The adventurer Thomas Dover combines opium with *ipecacuana*, sold everywhere as Dover's powders. Sir Christopher Wren injects a dose of opium in wine into the vein of a dog. The Abbot Rousseau ferments opium and prescribes his laudenum to the French aristocracy as well as to the poor. Tobacco excites polemics, prohibitions, monopolies and taxes. Coffee is forbidden and suppressed, prescribed medicinally, monopolized and finally accepted and taxed as well. The modern era approaches.

Monotheisms
with a Vocation for
Universal Empire

THE GENERAL HISTORY OF DRUGS VOLUME 2 PART 2

Figure 77 (previous page, from Volume Two, Part One). *The Temptation of St.
Anthony*, copperplate engraving by Martin Schongauer (c. 1435 – 1491),
British Museum. Known as the father of Christian Monotheism, St.
Anthony (c. 251 – 356), hermit and cenobite, founded a number of
monasteries in the Thebaid region of Upper Egypt. During his
first fifteen years of solitary life in the desert, he was beseiged
by visions and temptations which will later exercise a
decisive influence on Christian demonology.

Nohubo remedio.

Figure 104. *No hubo remedio* (There was no help), etching and aquatint,
Los caprichos [The Caprices], no. 24, Francisco Goya
(1746 – 1828), Museo del Prado, Madrid.

11
Theory and Practice
of the Crusade

For the destruction of the understanding is a pestilence, much more indeed than
any such corruption and change of this atmosphere which surrounds us. For
this corruption is a pestilence of animals in so far as they are animals;
but the other is a pestilence of men in so far as they are men. --
Marcus Aurelius (121 – 180)[1]

A.   **The Premises of the Argument**
   1.   **Judicial Logic**
   2.   **The Witches Hammer**
B.   **Sociological Reality**
   1.   **The Reign of Terror**
   2.   **Truth and Power**
   3.   ***Lèse Majesté***

---

[1] The Thoughts of the Emperor M. Aurelius Antoninus, tr. George Long. Boston: Tichnor and Fields, 1864 archive.org [hereinafter, AO], p. 230; among other achievements, the English Classics scholar George Long (1800 – 1879) was "the first Greek professor at the newly founded University of London" and "one of the founders (1830), and for twenty years an officer, of the Royal Geographical Society" (The Encyclopaedia Britannica, Eleventh Edition, Vol. XVI. Cambridge, UK: At the University Press, 1911 AO, p. 973); "It is impossible to rise from reading Epicetus or Marcus Aurelius without a sense of constraint and melancholia, without feeling that the burden laid upon man is well-nigh greater than he can bear" (Arnold, Matthew. "An Essay on Marcus Aurelius" in The Thoughts of Marcus Aurelius Antoninus, tr. George Long, with an essay by Matthew Arnold. London: G. Bell and Sons, Ltd., 1913 AO, p. 220); see also Leopold, J. H., ed. *M. Antoninus Imperator Ad Se Ipsum*, IX, 2. Leipzig: B. G. Teubneri, 1908, perseus.tufts.edu.

The Renaissance interrupts the cult of the other life and the other world. Man feels himself reborn because he accepts the natural universe as his home. Instead of claiming hypocritical allegiance to *I die but I do not die*, he asks to live autonomously for the duration of his limited existence. The divine (which Christianity had located in the distant heavens) becomes the immensity of *nature*, a source of infinite universes, impersonal by definition, which art praises and science investigates without anthropocentric dogmas, admitting the smallness of the Earth within a cosmic harmony.

The zeitgeist of this epoch is the legitimacy of the individual, the principle of self-government. Men awaken to respect one another taking reason as fundamental, understood as the free examination of things and their causes. In his <u>*Oratio de hominis dignitate*</u> (Discourse on the Dignity of Man, 1486), the Italian Renaissance nobleman and philosopher Pico della Mirandola (1463 – 1494) puts a speech (which vividly contrasts with that of Yahveh to Adam and Eve in *Genesis*) into the mouth of his *supreme Father, God the Architect*, or *the Craftsman*:

We have given you, Adam, no fixed seat nor features proper to yourself nor endowment peculiar to you alone, in order that whatever seat, whatever features, whatever endowment you may responsibly desire, these same you may have and possess according to your desire and judgment. ... Constrained by no limits, you may determine it for yourself, according to your own free will, in whose hand we have placed you. I have placed you at the world's center so that you may thence more easily look around at whatever is in the world. We have made you neither of heaven nor of earth, neither mortal nor immortal, so that you may, as the free and extraordinary shaper of yourself, fashion yourself in the form you will prefer. It will be in your power to degenerate into the lower forms of life, which are brutish; you shall have the power, according to your soul's judgement [sic], to be reborn into the higher orders, which are divine.[2]

---

[2] Bori, Pier Cesare (1937 – 2012), tr. The Pico Project/*Progetto Pico*, a collaboration

CH. 11 THEORY AND PRACTICE OF THE CRUSADE

It is not strange that, along with an astonishing flowering in the arts, technology and the sciences, this new attitude should provoke an opposition perhaps unprecedented in the annals of memory. From the beginning there are two fiery swords that block recovery of reason's autonomy. One of them is wielded by the tribunals of the Christian reformation, which in principle proclaim freedom of conscience but in practice defend a savage Puritanism inherited from the first Christian centuries, whose principles are salvation by grace and the shame of the human heart. The other is brandished by the Holy Office of the Catholic Inquisition which after losing power is reorganized during the Council of Trent (1545 – 1563) as the Counter-Reformation. Already in 1216 Pope Honorius III had approved the organization of the Order of Preachers (Dominicans); in 1233, Pope Gregory IX granted them the duty of annihilating apostates, converting unbelievers and submitting them to the Catholic hierarchy, faced with the heresy of the Albigensians (Cathars of Languedoc, in what is today southern France). In 1540 Pope Paul III in *Regmini militantis ecclesiae* (To the government of the Church militant) approved internal statutes (that reflect mirror-like those of the military) for the Society of Jesus (Jesuits) to join the fight against Protestantism.

The actions of both of these groups of vigilantes will delay for two or three centuries the changes demanded by this new spirit. They devise as an antidote against the Renaissance *plague* a body of doctrine and procedures that have incomparable importance for any historian of political tactics and the techniques of power. More than any other

---

between Brown and the University of Bologna, brown.edu., sections 18-23, (*nec certam sedem, nec propriam faciem, nec munus ullum peculiare tibi dedimus, o Adam .... Poteris in inferiora quae sunt bruta degenerare; poteris in superiora quae sunt divina ex tui animi sententia regenerari*); see also Caponigri, Robert A., tr. <u>Oration on the Dignity of Man</u>. Chicago, IL: Regnery Gateway, 1956 AO, pp. 7-8.

concrete necessity, to destroy legions of witches and to block their satanic movements will provoke changes in legal and substantive due process that will endure and be applied to every other crime, even to the liberal revolutions themselves.

For the same reason the crusade against witchcraft is not only the perfect example of how an irrational persecution multiplies to infinity a certain supposed harm but is also an enduring landmark in the strategy of social control, whose solutions continue to tempt governments even to our day. Until then there had not been invented a better system to enslave truth to the historical moment than what the Romans called the *merum imperium*.[3] Today, there is still no better database than that same crusade for understanding what might be called the *moral epidemic*, allowing us to observe the circumstances that cause a people to confuse a systemic aggression against their own intellects with infections of the air and plagues of the field.

---

[3] Ulpianus (*on the office of Quaestor 2*): "*Imperium* is either simple (*merum*) or mixed. Simple imperium is where an officer is in possession of the power of the sword for the purpose of punishing evildoers; when it is also called *potestas*. Mixed *imperium* ... extends to the power of nominating a judge" (Buckland, W. W. ed. The Digest of Justinian, tr. C. H. Munro, vol. I, 2. 1. 3. Cambridge, UK: at the University Press, 1904 AO, p. 66); the writings of the Roman jurist Ulpian (Domiticus Ulpianus, d. 228), "have supplied to Justinian's *Digest* about a third of its contents ..." (The Encyclopaedia Britannica, 11th ed., vol. XXVII. Cambridge, UK: at the University Press, 1911 AO, p. 567).

A.   The Premises of the Argument

The purification of the centers of paganism begins chronologically in France and Saxony, continues later in Italy and other parts of Germany, passing over finally to Spain, Portugal, England and the Low Countries, extending itself even into Scandinavia.   The techniques used by the Holy Office of the Inquisition are inaugurated in the Albigensian Crusade (1208 – 1244), assume a definitive form in the struggle against the witches, and from the thirteenth century onward repress a diversity of conduct, ranging from sexuality,[4] heterodox mysticism, Church reform, the customs of ethnic and social minorities, crimes of speech[5] and various other offenses.[6]   The Protestant tribunals came to cover an almost identical horizon and were especially ferocious on questions of witchcraft.   In Spain and Portugal for example persecutions concentrated on the so-called *new Christians* (Jews and Moors), who after having been obliged to accept baptism as the least worst option, were then persecuted for being insincere believers.[7]   In other territories the main contingent of those

---

[4] The Inquisitors judged cases of incest, lust, bigamy, fornication, soliciting (sexual contact), sodomy, and persons accused of intimate contact with animals (bestiality).

[5] These included blasphemy, speech and ideas. An example of speech would be the case of the physician Francisco Godios, a resident of Toledo in 1553, condemned to never more practice his profession and to receive a hundred lashes for saying in a tavern, somewhat drunkenly, that Cain would be released from Hell on Judgment Day (AHN, Inq. leg. 203/10, in Blázquez Miguel, Juan. *La Inquisición en Castilla-La Mancha*. Madrid: Pub. Univ. de Córdoba, 1986, p. 138).

[6] Under this rubric was included opposition to the Holy Office, reading forbidden books, possession of dishonest or heretical paintings or sculpture, Masonry, irreverence and the matrimony of clergy.

[7] According to the centrist historian José Amador de los Rios (1816 – 1878), in only the seventeen years from 1481 to 1498, according to the official data, 10,220 persons of both sexes were devoured by the flames (*devoradas por las llamas*) in Spain for

adjudged are the witches. But the judicial procedures (in these cases as in the others) were based on practically identical principles.

Promulgated in the eighteenth century BC, article one of the Code of Hammurabi states: "If a man bring an accusation against a man, and charge him with a (capital) crime, but cannot prove it, he, the accuser, shall be put to death."[8] Had there been a similar statute in existence during the Renaissance some thirty-three centuries later, the huge number of witches and wizards burned in the public squares would have been drastically reduced, and in Europe as in the Americas there would have been executed many Inquisitors, informers and

---

Judaism, with 6,870 more declared fugitives and 97,321 sentenced to confiscation of all their goods or perpetual prison (*Historia Social, Política y Religiosa de los Judíos de España y Portugal*, vol. III. Madrid: T. Fortanet, 1876 AO, pp. 491-492: *Limitándonos á España, sin salir ... ó cárcel perpétua*; by 1525, the truly fabulous (*verdaderamente fabuloso*) number of 348,901 Jews had been processed and condemned only in the kingdoms of Castilla, Aragon and Navarra (p. 493): *Hasta 1525, en que ... todavía penetrado*. The British Jewish historian Cecil Roth (1899 – 1970) admits that "[a]s far as Spain is concerned, the estimates given vary immensely (p. 143)" and so gives slightly different numbers in his A History of the Marranos, fourth edition. NY: Schocken Books, 1974 AO, pp. 143-144. Later, it will be the turn of the Moors.

[8] Harper, R. F., tr. The Code of Hammurabi. Chicago, IL: University of Chicago Press, 1904 AO, p. 11; in fact, the first four articles of the Code concern themselves with penalties for false accusation and false testimony. Article 2: "If a man charge a man with sorcery, and cannot prove it, he who is charged with sorcery shall go to the river, into the river he shall throw himself and if the river overcome him, his accuser shall take to himself his house (estate). If the river show that man to be innocent and he come forth unharmed, he who charged him with sorcery shall be put to death. He who threw himself into the river shall take to himself the house of his accuser." Article 3: "If a man, in a case (pending judgment), bear false (threatening) witness, or do not establish the testimony that he has given, if that case be a case involving life, that man shall be put to death." Article 4: "If a man (in a case) bear witness for grain or money (as a bribe), he shall himself bear the penalty imposed in that case (p. 11)."

bailiffs, equally incapable of actually proving the guilt of the accused. It is manifest that religious intolerance, prejudice and the mechanism of a feeding frenzy set in motion by the crusade placed Europe (just when the modern scientific method was being born) on a very inferior level of judicial rationality in comparison to that exhibited by the ancient Sumerians.

1.   Judicial Logic.   Before the epidemic of witchcraft was decreed, the investigation of penal cases in Europe was based on a system that did not admit confession as a means of proof. The magistrates used a complex mechanism of proof (direct, urgent, incomplete, distant or *accessory*, artificial, considerable, light, *et cetera*) that could only be combined or summed up within limits. Full proof would permit the judge to impose any kind of punishment, half-full only the punishments less severe than capital, and the light or half-proven a fine, understanding that two semi-full proofs were equivalent to a full proof and that two accessories amounted to a semi-full. It was a justice based upon the *absence* of the accused, which attempted to make up for it with the presence of documents and written testimony about her conduct, scrupulously arranged in order of importance. That neither the public nor the accused had access to the summary was based upon the principle of categorically separating the *sovereign power* from the *multitude*.[9]

---

[9] The French jurist Pierre Ayrault (1536 – 1601) supposed that the most immediate basis for this separation was the fear of the tumult, the shouts and clamors the people were ordinarily given to, the fear that there would be disorder, violence, and impetuous action taken against the parties and even against the judges (Ayrault, P. *Ordre et Instruction Judiciare*, book III.   Paris: *A. Cotillon et Cie/A. Chevalier-Marescq*, 1881 AO, part 3, section 79, p. 266: *Ce n'a pas efté la peur des tumultes, des crieries & acclamations que faict ordinairement un peuple? la peur qu'il y euft du défordre, quelqueffois auffi de la violence & impétuofité contre les Parties, voire mefme contre les Iuges*; see also *De L'ordre et*

Figure 105. Castration. Text from Eusèbe de Laurière's _Ordonnance des Roys de France de la troisieme race_, vol. 2. Paris: De L'Imprimerie Royale, 1729 gallica.bnf.fr, Philippe VI dit de Valois à Beziers, en Fevrier 1335, p. 109.

Instruction Judiciare. Paris: _Chez Jacques du Puys_, 1576, gallica.bnf.fr. and Foucault, Michel. Discipline and Punish, tr. Alan Sheridan. New York: Vintage Books, 1995 AO, pp. 35-36: "Before the justice of the sovereign, all voices must be still" (p. 36). The judicial basis was the infinite _imperium_ of the monarch, delegated to the judges.

But this system is hardly ideal for dealing with a plague like the witches, which demands proceedings adapted to the *enormity* of the crime and the *urgency* of the case. It was important to find a method of proof that could reduce the others to mere paperwork when it was considered convenient. Using as a foundation one of the principal Christian sacraments, it occurred to the jurists of the Holy Office to ask the accused for a *confession* of guilt, which vaguely could be based upon the ordeals (Sp. *salvas*) of hot iron and others, judicial duels, the judgment of God, even though they were a completely different institution. In fact, it would constitute the realization of the millenarian desire of the Church: the power to *solicit* with complete preemption from the faithful a declaration of their most intimate intentions; to dispose of souls without secrets, blindly trusting in the compassion and guidance of their legitimate shepherds.

The newly expedient proof could, moreover, be presented as almost revolutionary progress (for democratization) in the penal code. It would cut out in principle the privilege conferred upon judges to deliberate alone on the fate of the accused, while permitting that the accused should once again be part of the process, as had occurred in ancient law. The advantages of the discovery appear in a commentary made centuries later by that same French magistrate, who applied this kind of proof to common crimes: "It is not enough that the bad should be justly punished; if possible, it is appropriate that they should judge and condemn themselves."[10] The administration of justice gained in rapidity and certainty, correcting the defenselessness of the accused caused by not having the right to an audience.

---

[10] Ayrault, 1881, book I, section 14, p. 13: *Auffi, ce eft pas tout, que les mauvois soyent puniz iustement. Il faut, s'il eft poffible, qu'ils fe iugent & condamnent eux-mefmes*; Foucault, 1995, p. 38.

However, the way in which this proof collaborated in the just punishment of the bad was to introduce torture as a catalyst, as the key to confession, which was then incorporated into Inquisitional practice from the middle of the thirteenth century.[11] This implied the introduction of consequences into preliminary proceedings, in spite of the fact that from Hammurabi onwards the initial judicial process by definition had been a complex of testimony designed to determine if someone deserved punishment or not. Considering that torture appears in the Medieval law codes as one of the *punishments*, specifically

---

[11] "The methods of torment employed by the Spanish Inquisition were on the whole (contrary to what is imagined) conservative and unoriginal: the novelty lying rather in the assiduity and the recklessness with which they were applied. The commonest modes were the pulley or *strappado*, and the water-torment or *aselli*. In the former, the victim's wrists were tied behind his back and attached to a pulley, by means of which he was hoisted from the floor. If this did not prove sufficient to make him speak, weights were attached to the feet and, after being held suspended for a little while, the sufferer was let down suddenly, with a jerk which wrenched every part of the body. ... The water-torture was more ingenious, and more fiendish. The prisoner was fastened almost naked on a sort of trestle with sharp-edged rungs and kept in position with an iron band, his head lower than his feet, and his limbs bound to the side-pieces with agonising [sic] tightness. The mouth was then forced open and a strip of linen inserted into the gullet. Through this, water was poured from a jar (*jarra*), obstructing the throat and nostrils and producing a state of semi-suffocation. This process was repeated time after time, as many as eight *jarras* sometimes being applied. [Compare the so-called enhanced interrogations at Abu Ghraib and CIA black sites in the first decades of the enlightened twenty-first century.] ... The next torture, viz.: that of FIRE, is thus performed, the prisoner being placed on the ground his feet are held toward a fire and rubbed with unctious and combustible matter ..." (Roth, Cecil. The Spanish Inquisition. New York: W. W. Norton & Company, 1964 AO, pp. 95, 98). This treatment was renewed as many times as it was felt necessary to burn away the *negative*. The systems employed by the tribunals of the reformed churches were very similar.

as second on the scale of severity,[12] this procedure presented the novel characteristic of introducing the punishment of the accused into the inquiries needed to establish if one should proceed to punishment at all.

Judicial torture ... was included among the penalties; it was a penalty so grave that, in the hierarchy of punishments, the ordinance of 1760 placed it immediately after death. ... And, just as presumption was inseparably an element in the investigation and a fragment of guilt, the regulated pain involved in judicial torture was a means both of punishment and investigation.[13]

Thus, the differences between the phase of investigation and the phase of punishment, between inquiry and condemnation, between suspicion and guilt were erased. To get around this objection, it was adjudged that, after being extracted in the torture chamber, the confession would have to be reiterated on another day, not before the Inquisitor but before the judges in another location, presenting it as *possible*, *spontaneous* and *conscious*.

There remained a remote escape route, and this was the possibility that an accused would resist months or even years of torture. Confronted with such a contingency, the Inquisition established that torture should be *free* (without being submitted to trials of rope, water and fire), and that upon initiating the case the tribunal was authorized, in cases of singular gravity, to determine that torment would be done *with reserve of proof*. Such methods of proof were not subject to the meticulous gradations of earlier law, and they included,

---

[12] In the Middle Ages the hierarchy of punishment went: death (by various systems), torture, the galley, the lash, the pillory, exile and fines. The penitentiary is a creation of the end of the eighteenth century.

[13] Foucault, 1995, pp. 41-42.

besides the documentary and testimonial proof, certain special *indications*.

One such indication was the weight of the accused, because if a certain person weighed too little, or simply did not have a weight congruent with her volume, jurisprudence took this as a sign of witchcraft. Another was the already mentioned *satanic signs* (marks, birthmarks, points insensible and so forth). The third and most curious (recalling article two of Hammurabi) was the so-called *indication of immersion*. Tied by her hands and feet, the accused was launched into a large tank or pond, the reason being that:

Witches deny their baptisme when they Covenant with the Deviel ... [so that] when they be heaved into the water, the water refuseth to receive them ... and suffers them to float, as the Froth on the Sea, which the water will not receive, but casts it up and downe ....[14]

2.   The Witches' Hammer.   As a consequence of the expansive papal bull of Pope Innocent VIII (*Summis Desiderantes*, 1484), just two years later there appeared a work by the Dominicans Kraemer and Sprenger entitled the *Malleus Malleficarum* which summarized the inquisitional attitude. In this book they expounded systematically on substantive and procedural principles, formulating from diverse perspectives the duality drugs/eroticism. Its attention to questions of

---

[14] Hopkins, Matthew, Witch-finder. The Discovery of Witches. London: R. Royston, 1647, Querie 10, a reprint found in the Rev. Montague Summers' The Discovery of Witches: A Study of Master Matthew Hopkins. London: At the Cayne Press, 1928 AO, p. 56; see also Daemonologie by King James VI. Edinburgh: Printed by Arnold Hatfield for Robert Wald-graue, 1597 AO, ch. VI, p. 63. In essence, the suspect always ended up dead. If she floated (proof of her guilt) she would burn, and if she sank (proof of her innocence), she drowned.

psychopathology makes this work the oldest precedent for psychiatric manuals.[15] Torture is justified with these words:

For witchcraft is high treason against God's Majesty. And so they are to be put to the torture in order to make them confess. Any person, whatever his rank or position, upon such an accusation may be put to the torture, and he who is found guilty, even if he confesses his crime, let him be racked, let him suffer all other tortures prescribed by law in order that he may be punished in proportion to his offenses.[16]

This should not be understood as cruelty, since the more the witch suffers in her terrestrial life the less she will have to suffer in the other world. If she accepts with Christian resignation her punishment, and commends herself to God without hypocrisy, it is even possible that she would not end up in Hell. Kraemer and Sprenger also very much insist on the exemplary and dissuasive value that the public burning (Sp. *braseros*) has for the good Christian. Discussing the subject in some detail, Antonio Diana (1585 – 1663), clergyman and moralist, opined: "The Inquisitors ought to be more inclined to torture than other judges; because the crime of heresy is occult, and very difficult to prove ...."[17] Diego de Simancas (d. 1583), Bishop of

---

[15] However, perhaps the oldest precedent to our psychiatric manuals may be another earlier book in the same style, a forerunner to the *Malleus Maleficarum*, the *Directorium Inquisitorium* written by the Catalanese Dominican Nicholas de Eymerich, official inquisitor into the Albigensian heresy.

[16] Summers, *Malleus*, 1928, p. 6; Sprenger, 1574, p. 6: *Ipfam enim prope modum pulfant maieftatem diuinam ... per ferat poenas dignas fuo facinori.*

[17] Porres, Antonio Montes de. *Syma de D. Antonio Diana*. Madrid: Melchor Sanchez, 1657 Google Books [hereinafter, GB], p. 423: *Los Inquifidores deuen fer mas inclinados al tormento que otros juezes; porque el crimen de heregia es oculto, y dificultofo de probar,* citing Juan de Rojas (d. ~ 1578), Inquisitor in Valencia, in Ioanne a Rojas. *De fuccefsioniibus, De Haereticis, et Singularia in fidei fauorem. Salamanticae: Ex officina Ildefonfi à. Terranoua &*

Zamora (1578 – 1583) and counselor to the *Suprema* (Supreme Tribunal of the Inquisition), added a second reason: "Because the confession not only for the heretic but also for the Republic is beneficial."[18]

With respect to eyewitness testimony, the principle in the *Malleus* is very simple in that almost any person may testify to anything against anyone. It is not necessary to communicate to the suspect neither who it is that accuses her nor exactly of what she is accused. On the contrary, one of the recognized techniques is to read to the accused lists of charges in which all kind of inventions accumulate, understanding that to deny vehemently the most atrocious of these recognizes in an implicit manner the guilt of the others. In a doubtful case, the suspect is presumed to be guilty. Hence all kinds of testimony are accepted, including those ruled out by the law for common crimes including the testimony of criminals, the infamous, the complicit, perjurers, family, parents, minors and public rumor:[19]

Neyla, 1581 GB, *De Haereticis*, secunda pars, sections 295/296, p. 107: *In crimine tamen herefeos iudices ad torturam proniores effe oportet, & faciliùs ad quaeftionem veniendum eft, quia eft crimen fuapte natura occultũ, & facultas probationis de effe folet.*

[18] *De catholicis institutionibus*. Romae: *In Aedibus Populi Romani*, 1575 AO, title 65, section 51, p. 505: *Quid? quod eius confefsio, & ipsi haeretico, & vniuerfae reipublicae plurimum eft profutura.* See also Julio Caro Baroja, *El Señor Inquisidor y otras vidas por oficio*. Madrid: Alianza Editorial, 1968 AO, p. 38.

[19] Part Three, Question Four: Of the Quality and Condition of Witnesses: "Note that persons under a sentence of excommunication, associates and accomplices in the crime, notorious evildoers and criminals, or servants giving evidence against their masters, are admitted as witnesses in a case concerning the Faith. ... [T]his is true also of the evidence of the prisoner's wife, sons and kindred .... [S]o great is the plague of heresy that, in an action involving this crime, even servants are admitted as witnesses against their masters, and any criminal evildoer may give evidence against any person soever [sic]" (Summers, tr., p. 209); "When such an accusation is brought, any witness may come forward to give evidence, just as he may in a case of lese-

Figure 106. Woodcut, Forms of execution, mutilation and torture during the Inquisition (Germany, 1500s).

---

majesty" (Summers, tr., p. 6); Sprenger, 1574, p. 6: *Ad hanc accuſationem quilibet admittitur quaſi in crimine laeſae maieſtatis.*

An accusation levelled [sic] by an individual or the unproved denunciation of some zealous person starts the proceedings. But often a vague rumor can cause the judge to open a case. A child's evidence is considered adequate, and even statements made by personal enemies of the accused are accepted. The sentence ought to be straightforward, brief and final. The judge's powers are absolute. He it is who decides if the accused has the right to defend herself; he also appoints counsel for the defence [sic] and hedges him about with so many conditions that he is virtually just another counsel for the prosecution. Torture may be freely employed; and if the 'guilty' party cannot be made to confess, even under torture, her failure to do so can always be attributed to the Devil's power over her. ... Retraction and repentance are no way of avoiding the death penalty.[20]

---

[20] Caro Baroja, Julio. The World of the Witches, O. N. V. Glendinning, tr. Chicago: University of Chicago Press, 1971 AO, p. 97, citing the *Malleus Maleficarum*, Lyons, 1584, I, pp. 333-391, Part III, *Quaestiones* 1-XXX. Part Three, Question One. The method of initiating a process: "In answer to this it must be said that there are three methods allowed by Canon law. The first is when someone accuses a person before a judge of the crime of heresy .... The second method is when someone denounces a person ... but says he lays information out of zeal for the faith .... The third method involves an inquisition, that is, when there is no accuser or informer, but a general report that there are witches in some town or place ..." (Summers, 1928, p. 205); Part Three, Question Five: "[I]t is to be noted that a witness is not necessary to be disqualified because of every sort of enmity. ... [E]ven if other witnesses say that such a person has given evidence from motives of enmity, the Judge must not reject his evidence, but admit it together with the other proofs" (p. 210). Part Three, Question Six: "In considering the method of proceeding with a trial of a witch in the cause of the faith, it must first be noted that such cases must be conducted in the simplest and most summary manner, without the arguments and contentions of advocates" (p. 210). Part Three, Question 10: "[I]t should be noted that an Advocate is not to be appointed at the desire of the accused .... For he must not by any means conduct his defense as to prevent the case from being conducted in a plain and summary manner, and he would be doing so if he introduced any complications or appeals into it; all which things are disallowed together" (p. 218). Part Three, Question 13: "[A]nd in this case she is to be exposed to questions and torture to extort a confession of her crimes. ... And here, because of the great

Montesquieu (1689 – 1755) wryly commented:

Other judges assume the innocence of the accused; these always deem them guilty. In dubious cases, their rule is to lean to the side of severity, apparently because they think mankind desperately wicked. And yet, when it suits them, they have such a high opinion of mankind, that they think them incapable of lying; for they accept as witnesses, mortal enemies, loose women, and people whose trade is infamous.[21]

Alibis, in contrast, have a very limited value. Kraemer and Sprenger advise not to consider the testimony of a spouse as a valid defense since "it may happen that men or women are by witchcraft entangled with Incubi or Succubi against their will."[22] Neither should it be considered an indication of innocence the ability to bear torture, since this was often due to diabolic enchantment.[23] As for the variations detected in the declarations of the witnesses, this indicates nothing in favor of the accused, as long as they "agree in the substance of the fact, that is, as to the witchcraft, and that she is suspected of being a witch."[24]

---

trouble caused by the stubborn silence of witches, there are several points which the Judge must notice .... [U]nless God, through a holy Angel, compels the devil to withhold his help from the witch, she will be so insensible to the pains of torture that she will sooner be torn limb from limb than confess any of the truth" (p. 222).

[21] Davidson, J., tr. Montesquieu: Persian Letters. London: George Routledge & Sons LTD, 1891 AO, Letter XXIX, p. 94; Montesquieu, Charles-Louis de Secondat, Baron de la Brède et de. *Lettres Persanes*, ed. R. Loyalty. NY: Oxford University Press, 1914 AO, *Lettre XXIX, Rica a Ibben, a Smyrne*, p. 41: *Les autres juges présument qu'un accusé est innocent ... des femmes de mauvaise vie, de ceux qui exercent une profession infâme.*

[22] Summers, tr. Malleus, Part II, Q. 2, Ch. 1, p. 164.

[23] "[W]hereas others, who have from their hearts bound themselves to the devil, are protected by his power and preserve a stubborn silence" (Summers, tr. Malleus, Part III, Q. 13, p. 224).

[24] Part Three, Question Seven: "And if, as very often is the case, they do not

With respect to documentary and material proof, the possession of books included in the Library of Magicians and Astrologers[25] will be considered evidence of guilt, as is having certain instruments, fundamentally "glazed pottery stewpots, small jars, retorts, pitchers, sulfur flowers, crystals, bones, amulets, etc."[26]

The defense of the accused depends on the tribunal. According to Kraemer and Sprenger, the court ought to enjoy plenary powers. It will decide on a case by case basis whether or not the witch has the right to be defended, and in the affirmative, if it will be a curate named by the Office or a lawyer chosen by it. The time to respond to the charges might be hours, and rarely would last longer than a few days, though the usual (because of the great number of cases) was to have the accused many years waiting for trial in the jails. From 1488 the procedure is absolutely confidential in all its phases: "[A]ll the

---

altogether agree together ... even if it show certain discrepancies ... the Judge may ... decide that the accused is to be reputed" (Summers, tr. Malleus, Part III, Q. 7, p. 213).

[25] "Not content with the *Index Librorum Prohibitorum* published under the auspices of the Vatican at Rome, the Spanish Inquisition drew up and periodically reissued its own list of questionable works" (Roth, 1996, p. 191); "All books and writings in geomancy, hydromancy, aeromancy, pyromancy, oneiromancy, chiromancy, necromancy, or those in which drawing lots, sorceries, auguries, auspices, incantations of the magic art are contained, are altogether rejected" (Buckley, Theodore Alois, tr. Canons and Decrees of the Council of Trent. London: George Routledge and Co., 1851 AO, Second Part, Ten Rules concerning Prohibited Books drawn up by the Fathers selected by the Synod of Trent and approved by Pope Pius IV, Rule IX, p. 287).

[26] A description of these utensils, in accord with the jurisprudential Inquisition, can be found in Cirac Estopañan's *Los procesos de hechicería en la Inquisición de Castilla la Nueva*. Madrid: Instituto Jerónimo Zurita (CSIC), 1942, ch. 11.

parties concerned – the accused person, as well as witnesses, accusers, and officials, were sworn to secrecy."[27]

An expedient recognized in the _Malleus_ for obtaining rapid confessions is the formal promise to respect the life of the accused. One possibility was to absolve her in exchange for permanent services as an informer, in the event the magistrate himself could fulfill the promise. Another was to promise a reservation of time, supposing a more or less lengthy moratorium, before finally she would be led to the bonfire. The third method was to make such a promise to the accused, thinking to delegate to a different judge not beholden to the promise the function of dictating the sentence.[28]

Contemplating these measures altogether, never did they achieve so sublime a degree as even the appearance of common sense. They dealt with obtaining "plain and summary"[29] judgments, and this aim was achieved completely. With all that, before concluding an examination of this procedure it is important to mention one last aspect. As Montesquieu observed:

Having dressed them in brimstone shirts, they [the judges] assure them [the culprits] that they are much grieved to see them in such sorry attire; that they are tender-hearted, abhorring bloodshed, and are quite overcome at having to condemn them. Then these heart-broken judges console themselves by confiscating to their own use all the goods of their miserable victims.[30]

---

[27] Roth, 1996, p. 86; Cirac Estopañan, 1942, p. 226.

[28] "A third opinion is that the Judge may safely promise the accused her life, but in such a way that he should afterwards disclaim the duty of passing sentence on her, deputing another Judge in his place" (Summers, tr. _Malleus_, Part III, Q. 14, p. 226).

[29] Summers, tr. _Malleus_, Part III, Q. 11, p. 218.

[30] Davidson, tr. _Montesquieu: Persian Letters_, 1891, p. 94; Montesquieu. _Lettres Persanes_. NY: Oxford University Press, 1914 GB, pp. 41-42: _Ils font dans leur sentence ... à leur profit._

The mere fact of being accused justified such a measure, because justice could not treat in an equal fashion suspects and untouchable persons. The papal bulls laid out an effective system of financing for the prosecution, since not only must she defray the costs of her food while she passed months or years in the jails (exposed to every kind of blackmail by her jailers) but also the totality of her worldly goods passed to the Holy Office, and those of her family were submitted to exaction also:

Expenses were kept down by forcing the witch's family to pay the bill for the services of the torturers and the executioners. The family was also billed for the cost of the fagots and for the banquet which the judges held after the burning. Considerable enthusiasm for witch-hunting could be built up among local officials, since they were empowered to confiscate the entire estate of any person condemned for witchcraft.[31]

The *auto da fe* that concluded the process came to be considered a great spectacle, which competed in splendor and popularity with other celebrations. Thousands of persons, rich and poor, came from far and wide to attend the ceremonies of singular or collective burning, attracted by the indulgences and other spiritual benefits given to those present.

At Córdova, at one great *auto* held in 1665, nearly 400,000 maravedis were expended on the entertainment of the Inquisitors, their retinues, and the numerous guests. ... Another especially noteworthy *auto* took place at Seville in 1660. It lasted for three days, and was according to all accounts one of the greatest ever known, a throng of no less than 100,000 being reported to witness it. Forty-seven Judaisers figured (mostly Portuguese), of whom seven were burned – three of them alive.[32]

---

[31] Harris, Marvin. <u>Cows, Pigs, Wars, and Witches: The Riddles of Culture</u>. NY: Vintage Books, 1974 AO, p. 215.
[32] Roth, 1996, pp. 120-121.

Figure 107. Carving in nogal wood, *Juicio contra un monje o la quema de libros* (Trial of a monk or the burning of the books) Juan de Juni (1507 – 1577), Museo de León, León, Spain.

B.   Sociological Reality.   The   Catholic
Commissars and those of the reformed churches agreed on the value
of fire for purifying spiritual filth. The solution to all their problems
was a brave use of the bonfire, without the sin of scruples that could
only cause the evil to become exacerbated. The already mentioned
Diego de Simancas, for example, not only foresaw a simple end to the
witches but also various other degenerates as well, like sodomites, for
example, through the *brasero*:

They told me in Rome that it was impossible now in Italy to remediate or punish the
sin of sodomy. I responded to them that it did not seem so to me, but that it would
end if it was ordered and executed that a corrupted boy who would not denounce by
a given day after being raped would be burned [tr. gwr].[33]

That the boy might not have been *raped*, and that he might not have
been a boy, were possibilities discarded beforehand.

Having examined the judicial principles and the spirit of the
law, it is opportune to ask as to its practical results. Theoretically, the
only ones that should have gone through the purification by fire were
those who consulted witches, or who were witches, traveling to
diabolic orgies with the help of unguents, or casting evil spells and
other omens. However, from its very beginnings the crusade shows a
considerable exploitation, based on ethnic and class prejudices, when
not political. Joan of Arc (1411 – 1431), later Saint Joan of Arc who
manifested a temperament little given to lustful Bacchanals, was
questioned at her Trial of Condemnation about the mandrake root,
often reputed to be carried by witches:

---

[33] Caro Baroja, J. *El Señor Inquisidor*, 1968, pp. 34-35; *La Vida y Cosas Notables del señor
obispo de Zamora Don Diego de Simancas*, found in Serrano y Sanz, M. *Autobiografías y
Memorias*. Madrid: Librería Editorial de Bailly/Balliére é Hijos, 1905 AO, p. 171:
Decíaanme en Roma que ya era imposible en Italia ... después de violentado lo quemasen ....

Asked what she had done with her mandrake, she answered that she has no mandrake, and never did have; but has heard that near her village there was one though she has never seen it. She said also she had heard it called a dangerous and evil thing to keep; nor does she know its use. ... Asked what she has heard about the mandrake, she answered that it attracts money, but she does not believe it.[34]

In fact, critics, crazies and the poor were those who had the greatest probability of being converted into cinders.

Investigating cases of witchcraft in England, an historian reviewed more than a thousand investigations conducted in the county of Essex from 1560 to 1680. He discovered that the most frequent accusation, in statistical terms, came from someone who, after refusing to give a donation to a beggar (generally an old woman), attributed some evil to her later. Another generic source of persecution in practice was a plot of land in a certain area divided by opposing bands struggling for supremacy: one or the other of the factions sought the protection of the commissars, and from that moment began the exterminations.[35]

From the work of another historian, who reviewed the trials of witches in the southeast of Germany in the sixteenth and seventeenth

---

[34] Barrett, W. P., tr. The Trial of Jeanne D'Arc. NY: Gotham House, Inc., 1932 sourcebooks.fordham.edu., Fifth Session, p. 73

[35] MacFarlane, A. D. J. "Witchcraft beliefs as an explanation of suffering and a means of resolving conflict" found in Witchcraft and Sorcery, ed. Max Marwick. UK: Penguin Books, 1970 AO, pp. 300-301: "In Essex prosecutions the process seems to have been different; once a suspicion had arisen about a certain person future injuries were blamed on her. Someone first offended a neighbour, and subsequently suffered. ... When a person felt that he had angered someone, he himself felt angry and worried. ... The victim would feel justified in hating someone because she was an evil witch .... They almost always arose from quarrels over gifts and loans in which the victim refused the witch some small gift, heard her muttering under her breath or threatening him, and subsequently suffered some misfortune."

centuries, we know that the first persons accused were female, basically old women and midwives of humble status. During the peak of the massive burnings, there came to form part of the adjudicated, bar owners, some merchants and even a civil magistrate and a school teacher. In exceptional cases, informers incriminated doctors, renowned jurists and university professors, but the judges had no confidence in their confessions. This investigator could not find a single case where a clergyman or an Inquisitor was accused. In three processes it was a member of the nobility, though none of these individuals finished up on the bonfire.[36]

In Spain it was more frequent to accuse friars and nuns of witchcraft, sexual immorality and heterodox mysticism. Approximately ten percent of the 1,261 persons brought to trial by virtue of these crimes by the Inquisition in Cuenca (one of the most severe) were ecclesiastics, but none ended on the bonfire. A few were confined to their convents, and the great majority received acquittal.[37]

Along with the descriptive reasons for the investigations of witchcraft one has to add a kind of chain reaction, since torture extracted almost always from each accused the names of various accomplices. Moreover, soon the pecuniary and political needs of the repressive state became confused with the extension of the social plague. At the beginning of the sixteenth century, when the crusade was in its stage of apogee, Agrippa of Nettesheim (1486 – 1535), polymath, physician and occultist, denounced (in the face of severe

---

[36] Midelfort, H. C. Erik. Witch Hunting in Southwestern Germany 1562 – 1684. Stanford, CA: Stanford University Press, 1972 AO, p. 195: "In general it may be said that the first persons attacked for witchcraft were the most suspect elements of society, including widows, spinsters, and midwives. But as soon as a large trial got under way, the most vulnerable targets were the better known elements of society, like tavernkeepers and other wealthy men or their wives."

[37] See, for example, Blázquez Miguel, J. La inquisición, 1986.

danger) cases of bribery and extortion by judges and Inquisitors in the north of Italy, who took advantage of the fear of torture and the bonfire to obtain money from distinguished families:

A man who won considerable fame as a miracle-worker, for instance, Henry Cornelius Agrippa, spoke out against the immorality of judges and inquisitors in certain cases. In northern Italy these men had filled the minds of weak and simple folk with the fear of torture and bloodshed. They had extorted money from women of distinguished families, which inevitably provoked relatives to action.[38]

The same news was given by Pedro Mártir de Anglería (1457 – 1526), humanist and chronicler of the Indies, about a provincial Spanish Inquisitor known as *Tenebrero* or *Lucero*.[39] Thanks to the papal

---

[38] Caro Baroja, J. World, 1971, p. 109, citing *Henrici Cornelii Agrippae de Nettesheym. De incertitudine & vanitate omnium scientiarum & artium* (Leyden, 1614), pp. 278-279; Agrippa, Henry Cornelius. The Vanity of Arts and Sciences. London: Samuel Speed, 1676 AO, chap. XCVI, p. 330: "Thus while I was in *Millain*, feveral Inquifitors did torment many honeft Matrons, & fome of very good Quality, and privately milk very large fums from the poor affrighted and terrified women; till at length, their Cheating being difcovered, they were severely handled by the Gentry, hardly efcaping Fire and Sword." *Henrici Cornelii Agrippae ab Nettesheym. De incertitudine & vanitate omnium fcientiarum & artium. Lvgdvni: Excudebat Severinvs Matthaei, 1643 AO, p. 279: Hac cautela, dum effem ego in Italia, plerique inquifitores ... vixque gladium & ignem evafere.*

[39] Caro Baroja, J. *El Señor Inquisidor,* 1968 AO, p. 30: *El caso más ilustrativo es el de Torquemada. En un grado inferior, como inquisidor provincial, el de Lucero o 'Tenebrero' ... [con] la reputación de hombre impuro en sus actuaciones;* Lea, Henry Charles. A History of the Inquisition in Spain, vol. I. NY: The Macmillan Company, 1908 AO, pp. 206-207: "The hatred excited by Lucero had been too widespread ... It assumed at first the shape of an action brought by the chapter and city of Córdova before the pope, charging Lucero with the evil wrought by his suborning some witnesses and compelling others by punishment to testify that the plaintiffs were heretics. ... It was apparently the first time that an inquisitor had been thus publicly put on trial for

bulls, many became professional hunters of rewards. In 1545 Andrés de Laguna obtained a witch's unguent in Metz specifically from a bailiff, who had kept the product well hidden.

One has to mention also as an important cause, the phenomenon of identification with the aggressor, so beautifully described by Danish filmmaker Carl Theodor Dreyer (1889 – 1968) in his *Dies Irae* (*Vredans Dag*, Day of Wrath, 1943) about a merciless witch hunt in Denmark, and highlighted by the Benedictine monk Benito Geronymo Feyjoó y Montenegro (1676 – 1764) in his <u>*Cartas eruditas y curiosas*</u>.[40]

---

official malfeasance."

[40] Vol. 4. Madrid: *Por D. Joachin Ibarra*, 1770 AO, *Carta* XX, p. 257: *Finalmente debo repetír aqui ... que las prevaricaciones de la imaginativa, respectivas á objetas, que causan terror, y espanto, son sumamete contagiosas.* A skeptical investigator, Alonso de Salazar y Frias "attached great importance to the influence of sermons on the masses. He said that one sermon on the subject from Fray Domingo of Sardo in Olagüe, near Pamplona, had been enough to make the people there ready to believe anything. Elsewhere the Edict [Edict of Grace, a temporary pardon to all who voluntarily confess their own or another's sins] itself had caused children to start confessing and speaking of 'Sabbaths', flying through the air and so on" (Caro Baroja, J. <u>The World of the Witches</u>, Glendinning, Nigel, tr. London: Phoenix Press, 2001 AO, ch. 14, p. 188). The Swiss historian of art and culture Carl Jacob Christoph Burkhardt (1818 – 1897) wrote: "With the smoke of the fires in which the suspected victims were sacrificed, were spread the narcotic fumes by which numbers of ruined characters were drugged into magic; and with them many calculating impostors became associated. ... [T]he system of persecution had succeeded in permanently infecting with the delusion those populations which were in any way predisposed for it" (<u>The Civilization of the Renaissance in Italy: 1860 – 1878</u>, tr. S. G. C. Middlemore. NY: Modern Library, 2002 AO, pp. 368, 371).

CH. 11 THEORY AND PRACTICE OF THE CRUSADE

The unworthy zeal with which the legal proceedings were conducted, and the frequent application of torture, drove many unfortunate people out of their minds. No sooner were they accused than they began to believe sincerely that they really were witches and sorcerers. They confessed to acts of which they were suspect, in spite of the fact that they had not committed them.[41]

Propelled by so many various and powerful factors, the crusade was maintained at its height for more than a century. Along with the passive resistance of certain sectors and isolated individuals, a combination of superstition, intolerance, bad conscience, politics, greed, corruption and fear served as immovable pillars, as if the papal stimulus and the laws of each state were not enough.

1.   The Reign of Terror.   Pressured by torture or by an exaggerated feeling of duty or by an hysterical impulse, a man would denounce his own dear wife, a woman her best friends, a boy his parents, a brother his sister, a servant his employers. The obsession seized the imaginations of villages and isolated counties, which carried out the persecution on their own, with foreseeable consequences. Every kind of resentment found room to blossom within this surreptitious civil war. One of the vehicles to instill terror was children, favored witnesses in the courts. In Pamplona, two girls of 9 and 11 years respectively (pardoned by the Council 'given their ages' of charges that hung over them for witchcraft) managed to fill a jail with 150 witches in 1527, traveling the villages with the Inquisitor Fray Prudencio de Sandoval and four squadrons of soldiers. The process against the witches of Ceberio (1555 – 1558) had for its principal

---

[41] Caro Baroja, J. World, 1968, p. 213, citing Feyjoó, 1770, *Carta XX*, p. 257: *El mimio ardor de las procedimientos, y freqüencia de los suplicios trastornaban el seso de muchos miserables, de modo, que luego que se veían acusados, buenamente creian que eran brujos, ó hechiceros, y creian, y confesaban los hechos que los eran imputados, aunque enteramente falsos.*

accuser one Catalina de Guesala, who made her first declaration when she was eight years old. The trials of the celebrated witches of Salem, between 1688 and 1693, were also based on witnesses of roughly the same age.

If the judges did not respect infancy, daring to threaten children with torture and the bonfire when they would not inform, neither did the people demand anything better. While there were many women in a state of pregnancy brought to the bonfire, the village matrons took the initiative to put in stocks, hang from bridges or torture to death other pregnant women.[42] All this was done *ad majorem Dei gloriam* (for the greater glory of God) to combat a horrible epidemic that only in this manner could be considered containable. Notwithstanding, there is manifest in all this a case of self-fulfilling prophecy, and double play. First, due to the action of the civil authorities, preachers and various inquisitors, whose work caused a territory to become overcome with excitement, keeping it in a state of permanent unrest, the people accused one another of evils and infernal pacts. Second, by the role that these same authorities had throughout the trials, who had originated confessions inevitably adjusted to a prefabricated, stereotypical model. The process of inducing crime and afterward confirming it as part of a pattern appears exacerbated in cases where the same commissars and judges that intervened afterwards had preached beforehand to these same women the specific manifestations of the evil they were seeking.

---

[42] Caro Baroja, Julio. *Inquisición, brujería y criptojudaismo*. Barcelona: Ariel, 1970, p. 226.

2.   Truth and Power.   Is there in the structure of a society something that permits one generally to predict its response to magic? Is there something that can help explain the different treatment received by wizards in different cultures? One effort to illuminate the question comes from the anthropologist Mary Douglas (1921 – 2007), who describes three basic types of illiterate societies. In the first, which we can call traditionally well integrated, there exists a realist or just system of duties and rights that proportions to the individual an unbroken identity, prescribing what to do and how to do it in every situation. He that deviates from these customs is not a being to whom one can attribute evil deeds, but only someone who is unhappy. Faced with institutionalized magic, which is always white or beneficial, the marginalized perhaps believe themselves capable of doing black magic, but the tribe simply does not share their faith. For this reason, it is out of place in such a society any type of persecution.

The second type corresponds to tribes dedicated to commerce, with great social mobility. There reigns a completely technical and practical magic, oriented toward success. No individual has hegemony over others *a priori*, and each subject finds in himself his own meaning. In the future he has the alternative of becoming a *big man* or remaining in obscurity, and here in neither instance can evil persist. As with all the other members of the group, the wizard is not distinguished by being good or evil, but only by being someone who knows a profession and manages to live from it or not.

The third type, which could be called the traditional disintegrated, is where witchcraft shows up more often and with a decided ambivalence. Douglas gives an interesting description of this group:

Figure 108. *Scene de l'Inquisition* (Scene from the Inquisition), Eugenio Lucas Velásquez (1817 – 1870), Musée du Louvre, Paris.

It is one in which accusations of witchcraft are used to denigrate rivals and pull them down in the competition for leadership. The accusation would not have this effect if roles were clearly defined and rules of succession unambiguous. ... Here failure is neither ascribed to bad luck nor to the moral failings of the victim, but to the hostile, occult powers of his neighbour. Eventually the witch, whom rumour tries at the bar of public opinion, must either allow the village to split or clear his name in some ordeal. ... Witchcraft accusations are either used to expel unwanted members of the community, or to split the village into two parts, each part supposing itself to have thus sloughed off it dangerous elements.[43]

Periodically, such tribes feel themselves threatened by plagues of impurity, which provoke aggressive mobilizations by neighborhood groups, since in the name of white magic they try to exterminate the centers of black magic. According to Douglas,

Their exponents go round from village to village like a decontamination squad selling techniques for de-fusing potentially explosive human material. When they have made their rounds, the community sees itself restored (albeit temporarily) to a state of tranquil harmony. For as long as the spell lasts all suspected witches are rendered harmless and the witchcraft is under control; livestock will flourish, children will grow strong and not die till a ripe old age. ... But eventually a child sickens, crops fail and strife breaks out again.[44]

In structure and behavior, those tribes of Central Africa are the most akin to Medieval and Renaissance European society. If in both there predominates the paranoid or projective scheme of sacrifice (model A), this is not independent of the scope of corresponding rights and duties of each person also present in both contradictory profiles. Though money rules, these are not really mercantile cultures,

---

[43] Douglas, M. Natural Symbols: Explorations in Cosmology. NY: Pantheon Books, 1970 AO, p. 112.

[44] Douglas, 1970, pp. 121-122.

characterized by a great social mobility and an individualist cult of success, because the society values privileges that freeze this dynamic. But neither are they states in the original sense, linked to groups by age and sex, because an oligarchy rules over their different natures due precisely to its material wealth. They are, then, in the middle between the one and the other, without the social conformity that is based on the lack of ambition, and without the conformity derived from recognizing the right to accommodate everyone, without the cohesion derived from a basic equality and without the cohesion derived from admitting basic differences.

In the case of Europe, an area very much aggravated by social injustice, subsumed in incessant wars and catastrophes, there were shouts of *pharmakoi* like those used by certain ancient cities to purify their world. Considering the differences that exist between illiterate tribes and a complex civilization like the West, it is difficult not to admit without reservations the criterion of a Marxist anthropologist, when he attributed the hunt for witches to benefits of every kind for both the Church and the powers consecrated in the State.[45] To imagine that the entire crusade was a mix of political contrivance and the criminal delirium of the ecclesiastics (an invention supported by judicial aberration) is a criterion defended by illustrious historians early on. But neither this nor the practical advantages of a crusade exclude a complex phenomenon of *apostasy* or rejection of Christianity, in which there are at least three distinct though interconnected elements: a)

---

[45] "Preoccupied by the fantastic activities of these demons, the distraught, alienated, pauperized masses blamed the rampant Devil instead of the corrupt clergy and the rapacious nobility. Not only were the Church and state exonerated, but they were made indispensable. The clergy and nobility emerged as the great protectors of mankind against an enemy who was omnipresent but difficult to detect. Here at last was a reason to pay tithes and obey the tax collector" (Harris, M. Cows, 1989, p. 238).

older orgiastic cults and ceremonies of ecstasy; b) a practice of witchcraft of a rural type, distorted by the persecution and by impoverished, alienated and maddened masses; and c) the basic impulse of the Renaissance, exemplified by characters like Faust, who looks for knowledge and art deep in the *natural* mystery in order to live and enjoy more the finite.

3. *Lèse majesté.* All together, four centuries of the crusade suggest we should go deeply into the fundamental heart of the nature of crime and punishment. The Germanic peoples who divided Europe after the fall of the Roman Empire never professed a cult of *auctoritas* remotely comparable to that of the Romans. Their laws never were an object of adoration and they never dreamed of a right of propriety over the bodies and consciences of their subjects, in the style of Oriental despots or the emperors of Rome; on the contrary, they were named and deposed by popular assemblies, and stand out for their fidelity to their inherited laws before the pretensions of omnipotent power. It was Christianity that took up again the idea of a sacred royalty during the High Middle Ages, which ended up crystallized in the simultaneous appearance of an Emperor and a Pope, exemplars of reciprocally sustained institutions. The later reception of Roman public law, and the process that consolidated the absolute monarchies, would provoke decisive changes over time in their understanding of crime and punishment.

Most important is that everywhere the concept of *lèse majesté* infiltrates, with the consequent generalized institution of crimes that do not require a concrete, physical victim. For this reason, the foundation of the law that succeeded the Germanic is the assumption that "[i]n every offence there was a *crimen majestatis* and in the least criminal a

719

potential regicide."[46]   Because the king, the Roman pontiff, the *Escritura*, the monarch or simply the lord of certain territories was divine, punitive justice was based on repressing the *disobedience* to a superior, over and above redressing a specific harm caused to an equal.

This criterion explains something shocking for the contemporary sensibility, but undeniable in all positive European law from the twelfth century to the end of the eighteenth: *it is impossible to be an innocent object of suspicion*, as proof by confession begins with torture, utilized by lay magistrates in all kind of trials.   Only because from the Holy Roman Empire onward any delinquent offends first above all the *sovereign* (and in the second place only some such harmed person) can there be introduced and remain such an institution. Perhaps the process ends in a simple fine, but there will not be a presumption of innocence while there exists the possibility of disrespect to a superior.   And this possibility never disappears, because the force of the law is not the force of a common truth (was a blow dealt or not, a thing taken or not, a person who was or was not there), but the force of the regent, a man-god whom none may challenge with impunity.   Although there exists the possibility of never having attacked another person, there always remains *the part of the prince* in the accusation, the *affront* made to him by real or apparent disorder created in his dominions.   Even in the last third of the eighteenth century this criterion can be encountered intact:

Crime is a voluntary act committed fraudulently or by accident, in which one wounds the rights of another. I speak of *rights* because that act or that accident can be made against a *public right* or a *particular right*, even supposing that there is neither wrong nor injury to an individual, if one has committed something that the law has prohibited, it

---

[46] Foucault, 1995, pp. 53-54.

is a crime which demands reparation, because the *right* of the superior has been violated, and this has injured the dignity of his character [tr. gwr].[47]

If the Papacy inaugurated the use of torture in the inquisitorial process it is because witchcraft (like heresy) is the prototype of a crime against authority, where it is impossible to be innocent once accused. Lacking a real and physical victim, the victim is always the sovereign, and in these cases a true inquiry can not proceed. This follows from what a Roman jurist called *the right of war, the absolute power of life and death* that the superior exercised by right of personal *vengeance*, celebrated precisely in the place most frequented, as a public exhibition of his command. Only thus can one understand fully the invocation in the *Malleus* to torture the accused *though they confess their crime*: the witches are guilty precisely of *the highest betrayal against the majesty of God*.

The divinization of power, tyranny and oppression are the same sides of the same coin. It seems unnecessary to ask why in the crime of *lèse majesté* suspicion should always be equivalent to guilt. As well, there does not exist any other way to prohibit conduct that publicly might be considered monstrous, but which in private can be realized (and solicited) regularly. In this are distinguished the crimes of *lèse humanité* and those of *lèse majesté*, and from this one can verify (from the liberal revolutions onward) that the commission of any crime of *lèse majesté* necessarily implies a crime of *lèse humanité*. The affronted is

---

[47] Correvon, Gabriel Seigneux de. *Observations sur des matières de jurisprudence criminelle*, tr. Paul Risi. Lausanne, CH: *Chez Franç Grasset et Comp.*, 1768, gallica.bnf.fr., p. 9: *LE DÉLIT eft un acte volontairement commis frauduleufement ou par fa faute, par lequel on bleffe les droits d'autrui. Je dis les droits parceque cet acte ou cette faute peut regarder le droit public, & le droit particulier; car fuppofé même qu'on n'ait fait ni tort ni injure à l'individu, fi l'on a commis quelque chofe que la loi ait défendu, c'eft un délit qui demande reparation, parce que le Droit du fupérieur eft violé, & que c'eft faire injure à la dignité de fon caractere.*

mankind itself, as a species formed from individuals born with their own thoughts, free and irrepressible by nature.

But exactly because crimes of *lèse majesté* are crimes of thought, the modalities of their persecution present an almost perfect homogeneity across centuries and cultures. They never deal with punishing someone who murders a child to make a soup or for amusement, but only to assert that a certain minority (Christians, Jews, Maniqueans, pagans, witches, and so forth) do so habitually, as others take tea with toast. Hence the weight of proof is always charged with untouchable presumptions and others that ride roughshod over judicial logic. What we have seen happen in the crusade against the witches is identical in essence to what happened in Rome with the Bacchanals, where the lack of a *corpus delicti* was interpreted as proof that they were making the bodies disappear, and that the inexistence of spontaneous denunciations was solved by arbitrating strong recompense for any accusers. Reflecting on the accusation of witchcraft brought against a Zuni adolescent, Claude Lévi-Strauss commented:

By his confession, the defendant is transformed into a witness for the prosecution, with the participation (and even the complicity) of his judges. Through the defendant, witchcraft and the ideas associated with it cease to exist as a diffuse complex of poorly formulated sentiments and representations and become embodied in real experience. The defendant, who serves as a witness, gives the group the satisfaction of truth, which is infinitely greater and richer than the satisfaction of justice that would have been achieved by his execution.[48]

Certainly, in so many trials that which is pursued is not to clarify the truth of certain facts, but only to affirm the mythic/ritual system that makes possible the process itself. Hence the benefit

---

[48] Lévi-Strauss, Claude. Structural Anthropology, trs. Claire Jacobson and Brooke Grundfest Schoepf. NY: Basic Books, 1963 AO, pp. 173-174.

derived from manifesting evil exceeds the benefit of suppressing it, and for this one can affirm that the crusade from its beginning determined upon pure sabotage.

Such a fact seems consubstantial, not only with that but also to every business combating freedom of conscience through terror. Bodies might be incarcerated, dislocated and converted to ash, but thought is essentially refractory to coercion: the more one tries to repress it through external means, the more it embraces forms of resistance and delirium that invert the purpose of the censors (without going further shown in the Roman persecution of the early Christians). By the same procedure, certain isolated centers of pagan magic ended up being converted into a global cancer.

The witch that sucked the blood of children, destroyed crops, unleashed epidemics and cursed the establishment gave an office and income to various institutions, diverting the attention of the miserable and dispossessed to the guilty different from their oppressors, lending cohesion and legitimacy to orthodoxy, sustaining extreme forms of political paternalism, and, by definition, reaffirming a system of belief and hegemonic privilege, although one threatened with expiration. The case was that to capture those benefits the crusade caused the evil it really feared, which was an erosion of the *power of the sovereign*. The holocaust of innumerable persons (added to the prison and the economic ruin of many others) accelerated those secularizing tendencies, instilling in the soul of Europeans precisely a feeling of nausea and rebellion toward the commissars of *divine majesty*. For when the eighteenth century begins almost no learned person in Europe doubts that the hated plague would last neither more nor less as long as the procedures (invented four hundred years earlier) to suppress it so urgently.

Figure 109. Engraving, *Homme Condamné au Feu par l'Inquisition de Goa* (A Man
Condemned to the Fire by the Inquisition in Goa), Jacques LaRoque,
from Jacques Grasset de Saint-Sauver's *Encyclopédie des Voyages: Asie*.
Paris: Chez Deroy, 1796 AO, *Habitans de Goa*, p. 160/435.

Figure 110. *Capricho alegórico: la avaricia* (Allegorical caprice: avarice, 1852),
Eugenio Lucas Velásquez (1817 – 1870),
Museo Lázaro Galdiano, Madrid.

12
Christianity and Ebriety (III)

> *Therefore those err who say that there is no such thing as witchcraft,*
> *but that it is purely imaginary, even though they do not believe that*
> *devils exist except in the imagination of the ignorant and vulgar,*
> *and the natural accidents which happen to a man he wrongly*
> *attributes to some supposed devil.*[1]
>
> -- Kraemer and Sprenger,
> *Malleus Malleficarum*

A.   The Investigations of the Humanists
   1.   **The Inquiries of Laguna**
   2.   **The Observations of other Humanists**
   3.   **The Legacy of Paracelsus**
B.   The State of Things in the Americas
   1.   **Tobacco**
   2.   **Coca**
   3.   **The Instructive Case of *Maté***

---

[1] Summers, Montague, tr. The Malleus Maleficarum of Heinrich Kramer and James Sprenger. NY: Dover Publications, 1971 (unabridged republication of 1928), archive.org [hereinafter, AO], Part One, Question One: "Whether the Belief that there are such Beings as Witches is so Essential a Part of the Catholic Faith that Obstinacy to maintain the Opposite Opinion manifestly savours of Heresy," pp. 1-2; *Ideo illi qui dicunt maleficium nihil effe in mundo nifi in exiftimatione hominū. Etiā non credit effe daemones, nifi in exiftimatione uulgi tantū, ut errores quos homo fibiipfi facit, ex fua aeftimatione imputet daemoni* (Sprenger, R. P. F. Iacobo. *Mallevs Maleficarvm in Tres Divisvs Partes.* Venetiis: *Ad candentis Salamandrae infigne,* 1574 AO, p. 3).

When asked his opinion about what the *campesinos* attending the *aquelarres* were really searching for, the Spanish humanist, critic, philosopher and historian Pedro de Valencia (1555 – 1620) likened them to the *mystery religions* of the pagans. Although, he added, the essential attractions were ceremonies of unbridled eroticism, facilitated by the administration of drugs. His primary explanation was that the ceremonies were real and their purpose was the "desire to commit fornication, adultery or sodomy."[2] His second explanation was that these ceremonies were not real but only visions "brought on by the Devil with ointments, poisons and other substances."[3] Valencia even suggested that "all these vain images result only from the natural efficacy of the unguents" without it being necessary that the Devil should have compounded them at all.[4]

---

[2] *[Y] que haya acontecido así que hombres y mujeres perdidas, con deseo de cometer fornicaciones, adulterios y sodomías, hayan inventado aquellas juntos y misterios de maldad* .... (Valencia, Pedro de. *"Acerca de los cuentos de las brujas"* found in <u>Pedro de Valencia: Obras Completas</u>, eds. Manuel Antonio Marcos Casquero é Hipólito B. Riesco Álvarez, *presentación por* Gaspar Morocho Gayo, vol. VII. *León: Secretariado de Publicaciones de la Universidad de León*, 1997, *buleria.unileon.es*, section 3, pp. 257-258); Caro Baroja, Julio. <u>The World of the Witches</u>, tr. O. N. V. Glendinning. Chicago: University of Chicago Press, 1971, p. 181, citing *Discurso de Pedro de Valencia â cerca [sic] de los quentos de las/ Brujas y cosas tocantes a Magia.* Department of Manuscripts, *Biblioteca Nacional*, Madrid, MSS 9087, f. 262 v; *misterios de maldad* ... (Caro Baroja, Julio. <u>Las brujas y su mundo</u>. Madrid: Alianza Editorial, 1966, p. 230).

[3] *La segunda manera de entender* ... *en nombre del demonio son enseñadas a hacer venenos, ungüentos y todo lo demás* .... (Valencia, 1997, section 13, p. 269); Caro Baroja, <u>World</u>, 1971, p. 183, citing *Discurso* ..., ff. 270 r. – 274 r; *a visiones que les produce en un sueño muy denso que les provoca, mediante ungüentos, tóxicos y otras sustancias* (Caro Baroja, <u>Las brujas</u>, 1966, p. 232).

[4] *[S]e pueda pensar que todas aquellas imágenes vanas resulten de sola eficacia natural de las unciones sin que el demonio se las componga y haga* ... (Valencia, 1997, section 16, p. 271);

A. The Investigations of the Humanists

The first to be absolutely incredulous as to the diabolic nature of such celebrations (and the practice of witchcraft in general) was the Aristotelian natural philosopher Pietro Pomponazzi (1462 – 1524) who suggested in his work *De Incantationibus* that demons were not necessary because natural causes were sufficient to explain such phenomena.[5] At the time he was writing the book, Italy was overrun by a veritable epidemic of sorcery and decimated by the Inquisition.[6] Many "Catholic theologians and philosophers, especially Jesuits, saw his teachings as noxious and a potential source of heresy" and he was only saved by the protection of certain cardinals from a trial that would have ended in a bonfire.[7]

Following the lead of Pomponazzi, humanists like the physician, pharmacologist and botanist Andrés Laguna de Segovia

---

Caro Baroja, <u>World</u>, 1971, p. 183, citing *Discurso* ..., ff. 270 r. – 274 r; Caro Baroja, <u>Las brujas</u>, 1966, p. 232.

[5] Pomponazzi, Pietro. <u>Les Causes des Merveilles de la Nature ou Les Enchantements</u>, tr. Henri Busson. Paris: *Les Éditions Rieder*, 1930, gallica.bnf.fr [hereinafter, GBF], ch. 1, p. 118: *Les causes naturelles nous suffisent pour expliquer ces phénomènes et it n'y a aucune raison nécessitante de les attribuer aux démons: il est donc vain d'y recourir;* Pomponatii Mantva, Pietri. <u>De Naturalium effectuum caufis, siue de Incantationibus</u>. Basileae: *Cum caef. Maieftatis gratia & priuilegio*, 1656, AO, *caput primum*, p. 22: *Tertio, quoniam per caufas naturales nos poffumus huiufmo di experimenta faluare, neq eft aliqua ratio cogens haec per daemones operari: Ergo in uanum daemones ponuntur* ....

[6] *Au moment où Pomponazzi écrivait son livre, l'Italie était désolée par de véritable épidémic de sorcellerie et à ce titre décimée par les inquisiteurs. ... C'est le moment que choisit Pomponazzi pouir attaquer la sorcellerie* ... (Busson, H., *Introduction*, <u>Les Causes</u>, 1930, pp. 20-21).

[7] Martin, Craig. <u>Stanford Encyclopedia of Philosophy</u>, 2017, plato.stanford.edu; Caro Baroja, <u>World</u>, 1971, p. 104: Pomponazzi was accused of being an atheist and a heretic as he "did not wholly believe all that was said at that period about spells and magic."

(1499 – 1559), the Italian polymath Gerolamo Cardano (1501 – 1576), the Italian scholar and playwright Giambattista della Porta (1535 – 1615), the occultist Heinrich Cornelius Agrippa von Nettesheim (1486 – 1535), the jurist Gianfrancesco Ponzibinio (fl. 1520) who saw magic and sorcery as delusions,[8] as well as many others[9] carried their daring

---

[8] Ponzinibio's attack on the _Malleus_ "expressly denied that witches flew through the air or did other equally fantastic things" (Caro Baroja, World, 1971, p. 104); Lea, H. C. A History of the Inquisition of the Middle Ages, vol. III. NY: The MacMillan Company, 1922, play.google.com [hereinafter, PGC], p. 498.

[9] Another student of Aristotle, **Samuel Casinensis** (Samuel Cassini, fl. 16th c.) "felt that the Inquisitors had acted in a seriously sinful manner" (Caro Baroja, World, 1971, p. 104); Ristori, R. Biographical Dictionary of the Italians, treccani.it; Cosenza, Mario Emilio. Biographical and Bibliographical Dictionary of the Italian Humanists 1300 – 1800, vol. 5, second edition. Boston: G. K. Hall, 1962-1967, babel. hathitrust.org [hereinafter, BHO], p. 453; in contrast, **Paulo Grillandi** (1490? – 1517?), a "judge in many trials, mostly in the south of Italy ... gave the most detailed accounts of witches' covens .... Yet his accounts were based on sheer old wives' tales. ... [He] was so lacking in critical spirit that he unquestionably accepted a common tale about witches as if it was a factual account of something that really took place at a specific time and place" (Caro Baroja, World, 1971, pp. 105-106); **Reginald Scot** (1538 – 1599) published The Discoverie of Witchcraft in 1584, which "appealed for moderation ... [and] maintained that evil spirits only had intercourse with men in very exceptional circumstances, and certainly not the intercourse that was then believed to be common. ... Scot's book was burnt by the public executioner" (Caro Baroja, World, 1971, pp. 129-130); see also The Difcouerie of Witchcraft. London: By Henry Davidson for William Brome, 1584, loc.gov/ resource, the McManus-Young Collection (Library of Congress); **Andreas Caesalpinas** of Arezzo was "a radical after the manner of Pomponazzi" (Caro Baroja, World, 1971, p. 107); the Puritan preacher **George Gifford** (Giffard, d. 1620) was "arrested on a charge of nonconformity" (Stephen, Leslie, ed. Dictionary of National Biography, vol. XXL, Garnet – Gloucester. NY: MacMillan and Co., 1890 AO, p. 301) while serving in Essex, "a superstitious district, famous then and afterwards in the history of witchcraft" (W., "Preface," found in Gifford's A

to the extreme of mentioning specific recipes and reflecting on the psychology of the witches, guided by a philosophy of demystification. Part of their criticism of the policy of extermination is founded on demonstrating that the voyages of the witches were due to the natural effects of natural substances.

But it was not enough to prove to the ecclesiastical authority that these substances were known from Antiquity and used by the most famous physicians, because that would admit naked ladies fantasizing with exquisite voluptuousness or taking advantage of their disinhibiting effects to join orgies. Opium and the solanaceas were under a strict legal anathema from the High Middle Ages, and though the other drugs were insufficiently known by the Inquisitor, they fell within the taboo as *harmful potions*, *diabolic unguents*, or *evil herbs*. If in spite of everything some were used in the practice of medicine, they were used only under the protection of the professional respectability achieved by their dispensers, and always carried with them certain risks. It must be taken into account that until the nineteenth century there are in Europe a multitude of urban and rural *illegalisms*, that is, laws that simply are not obeyed but neither are they repealed, whose survival is little more than symbolic. For the orthodox, not only any kind of *voyage* but also euphoria as an end in itself, not to mention

---

Dialogue Concerning Witches & Witchcrafts. London: Printed for the Percy Society, 1842, reprinted from the edition of 1603 AO, p. vii); the Archbishop of York **Samuel Harsnett** (Harsnet, 1561 – 1631) made light of exorcists and "the strange names of their deuils" including "Frateretto, Fliberdigibbet, Hoberdidance, [and] Tocobratto" in his A Declaration of Egregious Popifh Impoftures. London: Printed by James Roberts, 1603 AO, ch. 10, p. 49, which "furnished Shakespeare with the names of the spirits mentioned by Edgar in King Lear" (Encyclopaedia Britannica, vol. XIII, Harmony to Hurstmonceaux. Cambridge, England: at the University Press, 1910 AO, p. 30); "Edgar: This is the foul fiend Flibbertigibbet" (Act III, Scene IV, opensourceshakespeare.org).

euthanasia, were of course abominable acts, deserving of capital punishment, which if the tribunals did not prosecute for witchcraft they would persecute for infamy *against nature*. We have an idea of what an orthodox Protestant of the Renaissance thought about opium with a story related by the German poet, dramatist and Meistersinger Hans Sachs (1494 – 1576)[10] regarding dead Turks after a battle with Christians:

... with astonishment they saw that they continued having the sexual organ hard and erect. The field doctor – showing no signs of surprise – explained that it was nothing extraordinary, since it was well known that the Turks were accustomed to take opium, and that opium caused sexual excitation even after death.[11]

It is for this reason imprecise to say that the humanists believed it possible *to exculpate* the witches by revealing the pharmacological basis of their operations. They considered the persecution criminal, of course, but they were conscious of the complexity of the problem created, for which it was only appropriate then to suggest solutions not being talked about, taking advantage of the fact that the massacre was beginning to disgust large sectors of society, even some ecclesiastics. The solution could not simply be the *innocence* of the classical drugs, but instead was something articulated in two parts. If the first was to reduce the supernatural to something prosaic, the second had to be to demonstrate that the prosaic presented great utility for everyone. Hence the work of Laguna, Cardano and Porta was as decisive for the

---

[10] Chisholm, Hugh, ed. The Encyclopaedia Britannica, vol. XXIII. NY: The Encyclopaedia Britannica Company, 1911, AO, p. 972.
[11] Behr, Hans-Georg (1937 – 2010), Austrian psychiatrist. *La droga, potencia mundial.* Barcelona: 1981, p. 61, originally *Weltmacht Droge. Das Geschäft mit der Sucht.* Wien/Dusseldorf: 1980; Sachs shows up centuries later in Wagner's *Der Meistersinger von Nurnberg* (1868).

first as that of Paracelsus was for the second. Only a combination of both things would be able to dissolve (slowly, over a long time) the millennia old identity established by Christianity between the pharmacological alteration of consciousness and the Satanic pact.

1.   The Inquiries of Laguna.   More cautious than many others, the testimony of the pharmacologist and botanist Andrés de Laguna allows one to qualify with exactitude not only the relationship of witchcraft with certain drugs but also the attitude of the epoch toward psychoactive drugs generally.

In his heavily annotated translation of Dioscorides' _Materia Medica_, Laguna spoke of opium, for example, as "a bringer of sweet dreams accompanied with all the happiness that can be desired,"[12] but

---

[12] Laguna, Andrés de, tr. _Pedacio Dioscorides Anazarbeo, acerca de la materia medicinal, y de los venenos mortiferos._ Salamanca: _Por_ Mathias Gast, 1563, book IV, chapter 75, _Del Solano que engendra locura_, p. 422: _Tiemplafe tambien por toda la Turquia de tal fuerte el opio, que beuido accarea fueños dulciBimos, y accompañados de toda la felicidad que deffear fe puede ...._ A man with the culture of Laguna would appear to be infected with superstition when he says that pigs intoxicated with henbane "die if quickly they do not drink a lot of water or if there is not nearby some crab they can eat" (Laguna, _Pedacio_, 1563, book IV, ch. 70, _Del Hyofcyamo_, p. 418: _Llaman la los Griegos Hyofcyamo, que quiere Haua porcina, porque en comiendo de aquefta planta los puercos, fe eftiran luego, y fe mueren, fi fubito no les echan mucha aqua encima, o no tienen alli cerca algun cangrejo que coman: con el qual cobran la fanidad perdida_).   Yet this remedy is hardly strange, since Dioscorides himself recommends as a remedy for the _Solano que engendra locura_ (_Solanum_ that causes madness) that one drink much aquamiel (honeyed water) and afterwards vomit (Laguna, _Pedacio_, 1563, book IV, ch. 75, p. 420: _Del qual tan grande peligro y daño, el remedio es mucha aquamiel beuida, y defpues gomitada_). As for the curiosity about the pigs eating crabs, while it sounds on its face like an old wives tale, "crustacean shellfish such as crabs and lobsters" can be infected with domoic acid, "a naturally occurring marine-based toxin that is produced by certain algae that grow in the ocean" whose mild symptoms include "vomiting and diarrhea" (California Department of Public

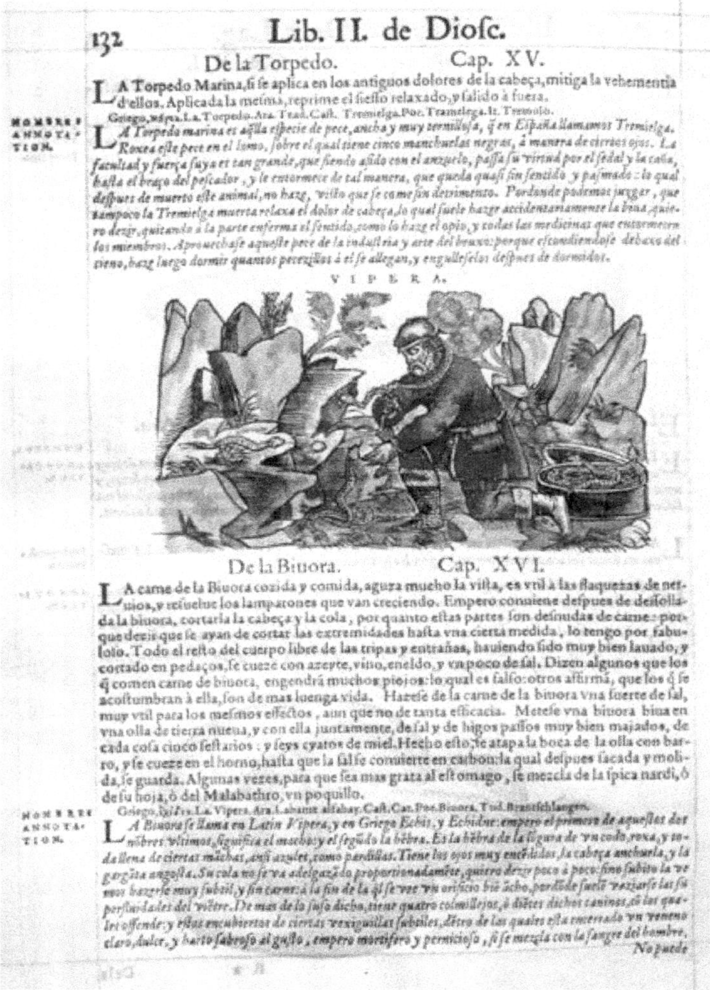

132 Lib. II. de Diosc.

De la Torpedo. Cap. XV.

LA Torpedo Marina, si se aplica en los antiguos dolores de la cabeça, mitiga la vehementia d'ellos. Aplicada la mesma, reprime el siesso relaxado, y salido à fuera.

Griego, νάρκη. La. Torpedo. Ara. Traa. Cast. Tremielga. Por. Tremelga. It. Tremolo.

NOMBRES ANNOTATION.

LA Torpedo marina es aqlla especie de pece, ancha y muy ternillosa, q en España llamamos Tremielga. Roxea este pece en el lomo, sobre el qual tiene cinco manchuelas negras, à manera de ciertos ojos. La facultad y fuerça suya es tan grande, que siendo asido con el anzuelo, passa su virtud por el sedal y la caña, hasta el braço del pescador, y le entormece de tal manera, que queda quasi sin sentido y pasmado: lo qual despues de muerto este animal, no haze, visto que se come sin detrimento. Pordonde podemos juzgar, que tampoco la Tremielga muerta relaxa el dolor de cabeça, lo qual suele hazer accidentariamente la biua, quiero dezir, quitando à la parte enferma el sentido, como lo haze el opio, y todas las medicinas que entormecen los miembros. Aprouechase aqueste pece de la industria y arte del bruxo: porque escondiendose debaxo del cieno, haze luego dormir quantos pecezillos à el se allegan, y engullesel os despues de dormidos.

VIPERA.

De la Biuora. Cap. XVI.

LA carne de la Biuora cozida y comida, aguza mucho la vista, es vtil à las flaquezas de neruios, y resuelue los lamparones que van creciendo. Empero conuiene despues de dessollada la biuora, cortarla la cabeça y la cola, por quanto estas partes son desnudas de carne: porque dezir que se ayan de cortar las extremidades hasta vna cierta medida, lo tengo por fabuloso. Todo el resto del cuerpo libre de las tripas y entrañas, hauiendo sido muy bien lauado, y cortado en pedaços, se cueze con azeyte, vino, eneldo, y vn poco de sal. Dizen algunos que los q comen carne de biuora, engendrã muchos piojos: lo qual es falso: otros affirmã, que los q se acostumbran à ella, son de mas luenga vida. Hazese de la carne de la biuora vna suerte de sal, muy vtil para los mesmos effectos, aun que no de tanta efficacia. Metese vna biuora biua en vna olla de tierra nueua, y con ella juntamente, de sal y de higos passos muy bien majados, de cada cosa cinco sestarios: y seys cyatos de miel. Hecho esto, se atapa la boca de la olla con barro, y se cueze en el horno, hasta que la sal se conuierte en carbon: la qual despues sacada y molida, se guarda. Algunas vezes, para que sea mas grata al estomago, se mezcla de la spica nardi, ò de su hoja, ò del Malabathro, vn poquillo.

Griego, ἔχιδνα. La. Vipera. Ara. Labamie alfabay. Cast. Cat. Por. Biuora. Tud. Brantschlangen.

NOMBRES ANNOTATION.

LA Biuora se llama en Latin Vipera, y en Griego Echis, y Echidna: empero el primero de aquestos dos nõbres vltimos, significa el macho: y el segũdo la hembra. Es la hembra de la figura de vn codo, roxa, y toda llena de ciertas manchas, assi azules, como pardillas. Tiene los ojos muy encẽdidos, la cabeça anchuela, y la gargãta angosta. Su cola no se va adelgazãdo proportionadamẽte, quiero dezir poco à poco: sino subito la vemos hazerse muy subtil, y sin carne: à la fin de la ql se vee vn orificio biẽ ãcho, por dõde suele vaziarse las superfluidades del viẽtre. De mas de lo susodicho, tiene quatro colmillejos, ò diẽtes dichos caninos, cõ los quales offende: y estos encubiertos de ciertas vexiguillas subtiles, dẽtro de las quales esta encerrado vn veneno claro, dulce, y harto sabroso al gusto, empero mortifero y pernicioso, si se mezcla con la sangre del hombre. No puede

Figure 111. Laguna, Andrés de. Pedacio Dioscorides Anazarbeo. Salamanca: Por Mathias Gast, 1563 AO, Libro II, p. 132.

Health Factsheet March 2018, cdph.ca.gov). While used as an antithelminthic, antiparasitic and vermifuge in Japan, the National Canine Research Association of America maintains that "[e]ven cooked crab shell is too dangerous for dogs to eat."

he is careful to warn that it is a thing done only *in Turkey*, without suggesting personal familiarity with the substance. Then he tells a suavely iconoclastic tale, in which orthodox protest alternates with the medicinal:

Henbane is that crude plant that we call *veleño* in Spain, whose existence should be well excused, because the world falls asleep and even goes crazy without it. I cannot complain of its birth, since I am not a little obligated to it as a repairer of my health. I say this because my brain had become so dried out, from certain temperatures in the year of forty-three that occurred at Metz in Lorraine, when, as I went more than fifteen days without dreaming sleep nor had the power to find a way to provoke it, there came to me an old Tudescan woman, who had the pretty figure of a witch, and seeing that the vigil consumed me, and had caused me to become frenetic, took a pillowcase and filled it with the leaves of this most valuable plant, and after filling it, put it beneath my head: which remedy was so certain and so prompt, that then I fell asleep as if sleep had been poured over my eyes. The truth is that, after having slept like a log for six hours, I awoke astonished by the action of the heavy and cold vapor of that herb, that to me seemed to have closed off the ways of my senses. In order to return to sleep a second time, I put between my head and the aforementioned pillow another pillow of wool, and thus slept with less heaviness, until, little by little, I came to restore myself to my natural constitution and first custom.[13]

Very common in Europe, where it grows wild at the foot of stone walls and in all kinds of ruins, henbane shows up in the Spanish refrain *al que come beleño no le faltará sueño* (he who eats henbane will not lack for sleep). In Castellano, henbane is *beleño*, and is the origin of the verb *embeleñar*, which the <u>*Diccionario de la Lengua Española*</u> has as a synonym for *embelesar* (to captivate the senses) while the <u>Collins Spanish to English Dictionary</u> has *embelesado* meaning spellbound or

---

[13] Laguna, <u>*Pedacio*</u>, 1563, book IV, ch. 70, *Del Hyofcyamo*, pp. 417-418: *El Hyofcyamo es aquella planta uulgar ... que poco a poco uine a reftituirme en mi conftitution natural, y primera coftumbre.*

enraptured. The Spanish botanist, pharmacist and chemist Pius Font i Quer (1888 – 1964) writes that the Romans called it *insana* and the Greeks *Diós Kýamos* (*habla de Zeus*, speak to Zeus).[14] However, while the Inquisition reigns, *embeleñar* is equivalent to *envenenar* (to poison).

The disparity between popular appreciation and institutional rejection feeds the ambivalence of Laguna. He pretends to feel offended by its existence (*cuya generation fuera bien efcufada*, whose existence should be well excused), but he recognizes that he owes the plant so much *como a reparador de mi salud* (as a repairer of my health). That *pues el mundo fe duerme, y aun enloquece harto, fin ella* (because the world falls asleep and even goes crazy without it) indicates neatly the stigma.

Similar thinking does not appear during the entire pagan era, where plants are medicinal or not, without even remotely suggesting political, moral or theological questions. Nevertheless, after covering his back with these digressions, what Laguna relates is none the less edifying. On the one hand, the plant reveals itself to be of great utility, and, on the other, this physician to the Emperor and the Pope is *no poco obligado* (not a little obligated) to the knowledge of that old woman *la qual tenia un lindo talle de bruxa* (who had the pretty figure of a witch).[15] The stigmatized therapy cures the consecrated, who has the elegance to recognize it. Instead of making a pact with the devil, there is the good fortune of an evidently useful medical practice.

Irony, married to compassion, also appears in Laguna when he refers to the antecedents of the unguent that he administered to the

---

[14] *Real Academia Española, dle.rae.es;* collinsdictionary.com; Font Quer, P. *Plantas Medicinales, El Dioscorides renovado.* Barcelona: Labor, 1982, book IV, section 68, fol. 119v, *Dioscorides Interactivo, dioscorides.usal.es.*

[15] Laguna, *Pedacio,* 1563, book IV, ch. 70, p. 417.

wife of the executioner,[16] obtained from a bailiff who requisitioned it from the house of a couple tried for witchcraft. After checking that it was without any doubt a psychoactive preparation, and highly potent, he relates what happened to the pair:

Being the salaried physician in the city of Metz, I visited the Duke Francisco of Lorraine, who was ill in Nancy, the year of 1545. In which occupation there came to his Highness an entire council to ask for justice and vengeance against two unfortunate old people, who were man and wife, and who lived in a small hermitage, a half league from that town, because (according to public rumor and fame) they were notorious witches destroying the fields, killing all the livestock and sucking the blood from children and had done irreparable harm. Hearing such bitter recriminations, the Duke ordered them taken and tortured, after which they confessed all that had been said of them, among other horrendous deeds ....[17]

As on so many occasions, rumor was enough because two old druggies ended by confessing so many horrendous deeds (*horrendas hazañas*), purged (for their own good and that of others) on the bonfire. But Laguna is not carried away by public rumor and fame (*la publica boz y fama*). Chronologically, the events he relates constitute the first demystification of the witch's voyage, where he also gives a demonstration of his proverbial prudence:

Said Dioscorides, who drank with wine a drachma of the roots of the Solano that brings madness,[18] it causes certain vain imaginings, though very agreeable, which

---

[16] Laguna, *Pedacio*, 1562, book II, ch. 27, p. 197; see GHD, vol. II, part 1, ch. 10, Christianity and Ebriety (II), p. 650.

[17] Laguna, *Pedacio*, 1563, book IV, ch. 75, *Del Solano que engendra locura*, p. 421.

[18] He probably refers to belladonna, though neither he nor Dioscorides speak but only of various classes of *solanvm*. It is in the Italian translation of Dioscorides where the expression *herba bella donna* appears (Matthioli, Petri Andreae. *Commentarij in VI.*

have to be understood between dreams. This then must be (so I believe) due to the virtue of those unguents the witches often grease themselves with, the great cold of which, of such kind as causes sleep for half a day and with profound dreams, imprints on the mind tenaciously a thousand absurdities and vanities, of the kind that after waking they confess they never did .... From which we can conjecture, that all the unfortunate witches said and did was dreamt, caused by the very cold beverages and unguents, which were so strong they corrupted the memory and fantasy, so that they imagined the deeds and still firmly believed them, having been awakened when they were dreaming .... These events cannot proceed from any other cause, but the excessive cold of the unguents .... Thus the stories, though they should be scandalous and merit an exemplary punishment for making pacts with the Devil, still the major part of what they say is vanity, since neither with the spirit nor the body ever did they depart from the home in which they fell overcome by their dreams.[19]

2.   The Observations of Other Humanists.   The

treatise _Magiae Natvralis, sive De Miracvlis Rervm Natvralivm_ (Natural Magic, or On the Miracles of Natural Substances) published in 1562 by Giambattista della Porta (1535 – 1615) is perhaps the most explicit text on the attitude of the Renaissance humanist toward the phenomena of witchcraft.[20]

There are two forts of Magick: the one is infamous, and unhappie, because it hath to do with foul fpirits, and confifts of Inchantments and wicked curiofity; and this is called Sorcery; an art which all learned and good men deteft; neither is it able to yield any truth of Reafon or Nature, but ftands meerly upon fancies and imaginations, fuch as vanifh prefently away, and leave nothing behinde them; as Jamblichus writes

---

libros Pedacij Diofcoridis Anazarbei de Medica materia. _Venetijs:_ _Apud Felicem Valgrifium_, 1583, AO book IV, ch. 69, _Solanvm Furiosvm_, p. 419).

[19] Laguna, _Pedacio_, 1563, book IV, ch. 75, _Del Solano que engendra locura_, pp. 421-422: _Dize Diofcorides ... del sueño._

[20] Porta, Io. Baptista. _Antverpiae: In aedibus Ioannis Steelfij_, 1562; "[I]n 1583 the book ended up on the Madrid Index of Prohibited Books due to Porta's naturalistic approach to witchcraft" (Stanford Encyclopaedia of Philosophy, plato.stanford.edu).

in his book concerning the myfteries of the Aegyptians. The other Magick is natural; which all excellent wife men do admit and embrace, and worfhip with great applaufe; neither is there any thing more highly efteemed, or better thought of, by men of learning.[21]

Porta also distinguishes clearly the fantastic parts of the recipes (which call for bat's blood and the grease of unbaptised infants and so forth) from the active preparations of the sorcerers. For him there are two distinct traditions: one derived from Medieval demonology which old demented women assume as their own through an identification with their persecutors, and another kind, empirical and *natural*, based on observations of botany and physiology, though the distinction was often missed by others such as the French demonologist Jean Bodin (1529 – 1596) who accused Porta of being a magician for writing down the Fairies Oyntment.[22]

The Fairies Oyntment itself is an example of Porta during his life trying to thread the needle between Inquisition and Renaissance. It shows up in the first edition published in four books in 1558. It disappeared from the second edition, reorganized, expanded, expurgated, edited and republished in twenty books in 1589. Thus, it appears in the French and Italian translations, made within a decade of the 1558 first edition but not in the anonymously translated English version of 1658, based on the second edition. Much had happened in the interim. "In 1586 Porta was probably again summoned before the

---

[21] Porta, John Baptista. Natural Magick, Anonymous, tr. London: Printed for Thomas Young, and Samuel Speed, 1658 AO, book I, ch. 2, "What is the Nature of Magick," pp. 1-2; *Bifarium μαγείαν ipfam dividunt ... vt Iamblicus libro de myfterijs Aegyptiorū haber. Naturalem alteram ... litertum candidatis plaufibilius* (Portae, Io. Bapt. Magiae Natvralis. *Neapoli: Apud Horatium Saluianum*, 1589 AO, *cap. II, Qvid. sit Magia*, p. 2); see p. 660, GHD, vol. II, part 1.

[22] Porta, Natural, 1658, "Preface," third page.

Neapolitan Inquisition .... Porta was instructed to abstain from publishing on divinatory and magical arts and write comedies instead."[23] As well, the *Academia Secretorum Naturae* (*Accademia dei Segreti, Accademia dei Oziosi*) he founded in Naples was suppressed by the Inquisition and forced to close.[24] In the first edition he repeated the recipe (at arms' length) which included a number of well-known psychotropic plants (hemlock, wolf's bane, belladonna) soaked in the fat of children [*puerorum pinguedinem*] which

they then thoroughly besmear over all parts of the body, previously rubbing them to make ruddy and warm whatever was cold and solidified. When the flesh is relaxed and the pores opened, they apply the fat (or the oil) to themselves so that the power in the juices can penetrate within more vigorously: these things are not in doubt. Then not on a moonless night through the air they believe themselves carried to banquets, music, and dances, and they lie together with the handsome young men they most longed for ....[25]

---

[23] Zalta, Edward N., ed. Stanford Encyclopaedia of Philosophy, plato.stanford.edu.

[24] Encyclopaedia Britannica, vol. VII, Constantine Pavlovich to Demidov. Cambridge, UK: at the University Press, 1910 AO, p. 966.

[25] Porta, *Pedacio*, 1560, book II, *cap.* XXVI, *Infomnia clara, & iucunda, obfcura, meticulofaque inducere, p. 85: Lamiarum vnguenta, Que quamquam ipse superstitionibus ... formosorum inuenum concubitus, quos maxime exoptant.* [See the complete recipe in GHD, vol. 2, part 1, p. 659.] Again, we have the problem of deciphering a non-Linnaen description of plants. The first ingredient (*eleoselinum*) probably "refers to hemlock and not to the harmless parsley, which it resembles closely. ... Hemlock is ... a well-known and ancient poison [that] may produce delirium and excitement. ... Aconite [possibly wolfbane] was one of the best-known poisons in ancient times ... which ... would produce mental confusion, impaired movement, irregular action of the heart, dizziness and shortness of breath. ... [*Sium* may] refer not to the harmless water parsnip but to the poisonous water hemlock or cowbane. ... Cases of poisoning associated with delirium have actually been recorded following the application of belladonna [deadly nightshade] plasters to the skin. ... Irregular action of the heart in

The cutaneous absorption of unguents, for example, occurred after previously rubbing them to make them ruddy and warm (*antea perfricando, ut rubescent, & reuocetur calor*) so that the power in the juices can penetrate within more vigorously (*ut succorum vis intro defcendat, & fiat potior vegetiorqúe*). Normally, this would have a limited effect

but there is no doubt that alkaloids can be absorbed when rubbed into scratches or into the quick of the nails, and it must be remembered that an unbroken skin is only possessed by those who are free from vermin and who wash regularly, and neither of these conditions would be likely to apply to a medieval witch.[26]

For the same reason, one must distinguish one group of users fascinated simply by the mythology ("[s]uperftitious, profane, and wicked men")[27] from another group for whom the potions and lotions serve specific ends, whether recreational or medicinal.

The faith in flights and other supernatural events of the sabbat not only derives from the hallucinogenic virtues of certain solanaceas, but also to the strong action of these substances on the judgment even after they have awoken from the trance. Depending on the proportions in which they are used, the solanaceas and other drugs (opium, cannabis, speckled flour, psychoactive mushrooms), the experience induced can be diametrically opposite. Chiefly, it is important to take into account the cultural background of the subject, the propensity for hysteria, depression, etc. The daring demystification

---

a person falling asleep produces the well-known sensation of suddenly falling through space, and it seems quite possible that the combination ... might produce the sensation of flying (Clark, A. J. "Appendix V – Flying Ointments" found in Murray, Margaret Alice. The Witch-Cult in Western Europe. Oxford: at the Clarendon Press, 1921 AO, pp. 279-280).

[26] Clark, in Murray (1921), p. 280.

[27] Porta, Natural Magick, 1658, Book I, ch. 2, p. 2 "What is the Nature of Magick.".

of Porta leads him to suggest careful trials with these types of preparations, always accounting for a diversity of response:

> I think it opportune to say, toward the end of not discouraging those who experiment, that these things do not function the same way for everyone: among others, melancholics, whose nature is depressive and cold, may experience fewer effects.[28]

The *epidemic* of witchcraft is, then, something created by the suggestion of the persecutors and the credulity of the persecuted, a combination of intolerance and barbarity in nearly equal doses. As none of this was acceptable, only the prudence of Laguna will save him from suffering; Pomponazzi, Cardano, Porta, Agrippa de Nettesheim and Ponzibinio, among others, will test in differing degrees the consequences of disturbing the foundations of the crusade, and many copies of the work of Laguna will be excised by the Inquisition of paragraphs and entire pages dedicated to the poppy and the solanaceas.

Among the group of dissidents with respect to the crusade, one must include also the Dutch physician and occultist Jan de Wier (Johannes Weyer, 1515 – 1588), although his is a special case. In fact, Wier (who Bodin argued with on this point)[29] proposed to treat the witches like mad women, prefiguring the posture that today is defended for the users of illegal drugs. He expressly urged the European authorities that they should consider those accused of practicing witchcraft as *sick and insane*. Naturally, it was less savage to intern these people in lunatic asylums than to toast them in the public

---

[28] Porta, Jean Baptiste. *La Magie Naturelle*. Roven: Chez Jacques Lucas, 1680 GBF (*Bibliothèque nationale de France*), *Livre Second, chapitre XXVI*, pp. 385-386: *Davantage encore j'eftime convenable ... d'un nature fort froide & frilleufe, & la vaporation d'iceux eft petite ...*

[29] "*Refvtation des opinions de Jean Wier*," in Jean Bodin's *De la Demonomanie des Sorciers*. Paris: *Chez Iacqves Dv-Pvys*, 1587 AO, pp. 238 - 277.

square. But Wier considered the phenomenon with a partiality almost as notable as the Inquisitors, and far from the attitude of the other humanists. The posture he defended is expressed in the title of his 1583 work, _De Praestigiis Daemonum, & Incantationibus ac Veneficiis_ (On the Illusions of the Demons and on Spells and Poisons)[30] where he limited himself to denouncing practices of swindling and cases of simple idiocy, without going deeper into the pharmacology and politics of the subject. Though a certain proportion of those accused of witchcraft were effectively simply more or less incurably mad, it is no less certain that in the phenomenon there were elements of paganism, pharmacological experimentation and the rejection of the reigning spiritual orthodoxy; many, like the _campesinos_, only attended archaic ceremonies which the Christian catequism had progressively deformed with its persecution. To lock up these people in lunatic asylums was like trading the horror of the bonfire for that of permanent straight jacket and other tortures of the loony bin.

Up to what point there is in Wier (under the varnish of humanism) a mix of historical determinism [the Ottoman Empire was then assaulting the walls of Vienna] and ignorance of classical medicine is indicated in his own observations on opium. Speaking of the Turks and the Persians, in another section of the work, he explains the Muslim habit of taking the drug "because they think that in eating it they become very strong and they do not fear so much the dangers of war."[31] The same explanation was echoed by another contemporary,

---

[30] In Wieri, Ioannis. _Opera Omnia._ Amstelodami: _Apud Petrum Vanden Berge_, 1660 AO, p. 1 _et seq._

[31] Wier, Iean. _Histoires Dispvtes et Discovrs: Des Illvsions et impostvres des diables, des magiciens infames, sorcieres et empoisonnevrs,_ tr. Iaques Grevin, vol. I. Paris: _Aux Bureaux du Progrès Médical/ A. Delahaye et Lecrosnier,_ 1885 AO, _Livre_ III, ch. XVIII, De l'opion, p. 383: _pourautant qu'ils penfent qu'en le mangeant ils deuiennent plus forts, & que moins ils craignent les dangers de la guerre;_ Wieri, _Opera,_ 1660, _De praestigiis daemonum,_ liber tertius,

the French traveler, naturalist and diplomat Pierre Belon du Mans (1517 – 1564), who also writes that the reason they eat it is that they believe that they become more valiant and fear less the perils of battle.[32]

Beyond the attempt to fix the Turkish success in battle on their appetite for opium, another favorite explanation was that alluded to earlier, that Muslim men used opium to enhance their ability to achieve erections. This will provoke an express denial on the part of the Portuguese herbalist, ethnobotanist and physician to the Viceroy of Goa, Garcia da Orta (1490? – 1570?) in his _Coloquios dos Simples e Drogas da India_ (1563). Da Orta, who deeply knew the East, presented much of the book as a dialogue between himself and a fabricated Dr. Ruano. About opium and lust, he comments:

ORTA

The Amfiam is the opium, and as for its being much used to eat among many people, it is really eaten in small quantity, though much is required in trade to supply all the things it is in demand for. ...

RUANO

And they do not take it as a luxury as they told me, for this is against all medicine and reason if it is efficacious for the work of Venus.

ORTA

There is much reason in what you say, for it is not efficacious in that way but rather harmful .... All learned physicians tell me that it makes a man impotent, and soon makes Venus take leave of him. ...

---

cap. XVIII, _De opio_, p. 225: _quod eo vorato fe valiores effe, minufque belli pericula timere, perfuafum habeant._

[32] _Les Observations de Plvsievrs Singvlaritez et Choses Memorables_. Paris: _Chez Hierofme de Marnef_, 1588 AO, p. 405: _La raifon pourquoy ilz en mangent, eft qu'ilz fe perfuadét en eftre plus vaillans, & craindre monis les perilz de la guerre._

CH. 12 CHRISTIANITY AND EBRIETY (III)

RUANO

But so many people use it for fleshly lusts, they cannot all be deceived. ...

ORTA

The imagination respecting the effect of anything helps much in carnal lusts .... As those who take opium are beside themselves, the act of Venus comes more slowly. Many females do not give the seed quickly, and when the man is slow, the female also reaches the act of Venus more slowly, so that they both complete the act at one time.[33]

Beginning with the humanists, plants and the drugs made from them begin to be demystified. Opium, for example, and the Turkish propensity to consume it, is no longer blamed for post-mortem priapism, battlefield victories or augmented lust. Now, European culture completely coincides with the opinion of the philosopher and mathematician Michel Eyquem de Montaigne (1533 – 1592) concerning witchcraft and diabolic herbs: "After all, 'tis setting a man's conjectures at a very high price, upon them to cause a man to be roasted alive."[34]

The year that Montaigne died Pierre Gassendi (1592 – 1655) was born, a strange combination of cleric, mathematician and Epicurean philosopher who clearly manifests this change of attitude. Gassendi [so the story goes]

---

[33] Orta, Garcia da. <u>Colloquies on the Simples & Drugs of India</u>, tr. Sir Clements Markham, ed. Conde de Ficalho. London: Henry Sotheran and Co., 1913 AO, pp. 331-332; *O amfiam he o opio, e por ser muyto usado ... E não o tomam pera a luxuria ... e em hum tempo juntamente ...* (<u>*Coloquios dos Simples E Drogas Da India*</u>, ed. Conde de Ficalho, vol. II. Lisboa: *Imprensa Nacional*, 1892 AO, pp. 171-2).

[34] <u>Essays of Montaigne</u>, tr. Charles Cotton, vol. III. London: Reeves and Turner, 1877 AO, Book III, ch. 11, Of Cripples, p. 333; *Apres tout, ceft mettre fes coniectures à bien haut prix, que d'en faire cuire vn homme tout vif* (<u>*Les Essais de Michel, Seignevr de Montaigne*</u>. Paris: Chez Charles Angot, 1657 GBF, *Livre* III, *chapitre* XI, *Des Boiteux*, p. 768).

gave a narcotic [not an unguent] to several villagers living in the Basse Alpes and told them they were going to a 'Sabbath'. This potion had been made up from a recipe given to Gassendi by a sorcerer. The villagers fell into a deep sleep and when they fully regained consciousness, they related a series of things they had seen. The defender of epicureanism was thus able to prove that the usually accepted view of witchcraft was wrong.[35]

This explanation, that begins to become majority opinion, is observed in a comedy by the Spanish dramatist Francisco de Rojas Zorrilla (1607 – 1648), *Lo que queria ver el Marqués de Villena*, where the following dialog appears between the Marquis (a man accused in his time of witchcraft) and the clown Zambapalo:

MARQUIS
Then others believe that the witches fly.

ZAMBAPALO
They don't?

MARQUIS
No, ignorant one.

---

[35] Caro Baroja, World, 1971, p. 205. The author admits, however, that he is "unable to give a concrete reference to the work in which Gassendi speaks of his experiment but it is quoted by Tissot, etc. (p. 299)." Yet his cite (Tissot, J. *L'Imagination, Ses Bienfaits et Ses Egarement surtout dans le Domaine du Marveilleux*. Paris: Didier et Cie, 1868) contains no searchable mention of Gassendi. Larousse does include the tale: *S'étant rendu dans une vallée des Basses-Alpes, où la sorcellerie ... étaient le résultat d'une veritable aliénation mentale* (Larousse, Pierre. *Grand Dictionnaire Universel du XIXe Siècle*, vol. 14. Paris: Administration de Grand Dictionnaire Universel, 1875 AO, *Sorcellerie*, p. 891). The story, though instructive, illustrative of his philosophy and beloved by certain university survey course instructors, remains, so far, unverified with a primary source.

Figure 112. *Mucho hay que chupar* (There is plenty to suck), *Los caprichos* (The Caprices), no. 45, aquatint and etching, Francisco Goya (1746 – 1828), Museo del Prado, Madrid.

ZAMBAPALO
I ask myself how it is that I am such a fool.

MARQUIS
They annoint themselves.

ZAMBAPALO
And then?

MARQUIS
That ointment, which is of
Opium and henbane,
Provokes a dream,
That the demon offers them,
Of such quality, that it appears
True that which was dreamt.[36]

The dramatist and poet Pedro Calderón de la Barca (1600 – 1681), one of the mentors of Rojas Zorrilla, also included in his _La vida es sueño_ (Life is a Dream) three verses on the plants used as a base of the witch's potions.[37] The same can be observed in the theological treatise _De la Recherche de la Vérité_ (On the Search for the Truth) by the Cartesian philosopher Nicolas Malebranche (1638 – 1715) which insists on the simple vegetal action of the witch's potions and the

---

[36] Rojas Zorrilla, Francisco de. _Lo que queria ver el Marqués de Villena_, found in _Biblioteca de Autores Españoles, Comedias Escogidas_, ed. Ramón de Mesonero Romanos. Madrid: Imprenta de Hernando y Compania, 1897 AO, pp. 330-331: _Luego otros que creen que vuelan las brujas ... Que es verdad lo que fué sueño._
[37] Calderón de la Barca, Pedro. _La Vida es Sueno_. Madrid: Librerias de la Viuda É Hijos de Cuesta, 1881 AO, _Jornada Segunda_, p. 50: _Con la bebida, en efecto,/ Que es el opio, la adormidera/ Y el beleno compusieron_ (with the drink, in fact, which is composed of the opium poppy and henbane).

Figure 113. *Ensayos* (Trials), *Los caprichos* (The Caprices), no. 60,
aquatint and etching, Francisco Goya (1746 – 1828),
Museo del Prado, Madrid.

purely imaginary nature of the voyage, often through prior suggestion.[38]

Though the burnings continue at their apogee through the middle of the seventeenth century (when the text of Malebranche appears), practically all the writers coincide in a demystification of the sinister cauldron of the witches. Now one speaks with frankness of specific substances (*medicines, toxins, drugs*) and which ones in which cases; after centuries of silence and whispers, one can hear again the names of opium, cannabis, henbane, mandrake, etc. Of course, the dogmatic ecclesiastical official continued to believe that witches really could fly, cause hailstorms or massive crimes at a distance, and so maintained the Inquisitional presumption that their potions and lotions were an irrefutable proof of satanic pacts. However, *apostasy* has lost a large part of its mystery and, with it, something of its absolute malignity. After enjoying a majoritarian acceptance among the clergy, the Thomist theory of the physical intervention of Satan in nature is abandoned in favor of the Augustinian *diabolic illusion*, more in agreement with the pharmacological basis of the supposed phenomenon.

---

[38] Malebranche, Nicolas. *De la Recherche de la Vérité*, found in *Oeuvres de Malebranche*, vol. III, ed. Jules Simon. Paris: Charpentier et Cie, 1871 AO, book II, part three, ch. 6, p. 332: *Ils se frottent de certaine drogue dans ce dessein, ils se couchent; cette disposition de leur coeur échauffe encore leur imagination ... pour leur faire juger, dans le sommeil, comme présents tous les mouvements de la cérémonie dont il leur avait fait la description* (they rub themselves with a certain drug with the intention [of attending a sabbat] and they go to bed. The disposition of the heart heats even more the imagination ... to make them judge, during the dream, as real all the movements of the ceremony of which they had been given a description).

3.   The Legacy of Paracelsus.   The birth of an official pharmacology, *white*, which assimilated not only the classical practices but also the complex of the *black* discoveries produced during the Middle Ages is chiefly the work of the Swiss physician and alchemist, Philippus Aureolus Theophrastus Bombastus von Hohenheim, aka Paracelsus (1493/4 – 1541).   If the humanists highlighted the natural virtues of lotions and potions used by the witches, the school of Basel will maintain that some of their ingredients, and even some of their specific recipes, would allow for a major advance in medicine.

When Paracelsus began to show up as the principal European therapeutic authority, a good part of the herbalists already used the remedies of the *curanderas*, lightly altered only in their presentation; instead of administering them as unguents and philters they appear in the form of pills, syrups and tinctures. That their content differed little from that of the diabolic unguents, one can judge by the recipe of one of the medicines considered a scientific novelty at the beginning of the seventeenth century, the tablets of Rofcellus for sleeping. Its formula is enumerated by the Flemish physician Carel Batens (1640 – 1617) in his so-called <u>*Secreet-Boeck*</u>:

Take the rinds of Mandrake roots one handfull, Henbane feed one ounce, white and red Poppy feed, of each one ounce. Bruife all thefe and boyl them in two pound of Fountain water, untill a third part be confumed, then drain it, and add the whiteft Sugar one pound, and when they are again boyl'd almoft to the perfect confiftence of Sugar, adde Nutmegs, Galla Mofchata, Lignum Aloes of each two drams, bark of Mandrake, feed of Henbane, feeds of red and white Poppy, of each three drams, Opium two drams, make tables according to Art. *Rofcellus.*[39]

---

[39] Wecker, John et al. <u>Eighteen Books of the Secrets of Art & Nature</u>. London: Simon Miller, 1660 GB, Book V, ch. 9, Of Sleep, p. 105; *Neenzt Schorffen van den wortel van Mandragora/ een hant bol ... Opium, twee draghmen/ maecht hier van platte koecrkens/ na*

Figure 114. *A caza de dientes* (Out hunting for teeth), *Los caprichos*
(The Caprices), no. 12, aquatint and etching, Francisco
Goya (1746 – 1828), Museo del Prado, Madrid.

---

de konste. Rofcellus (Battum, Carolum. *Secreet-Boeck Van veel diverfche en Heerlijcke Konften in veelderleye Materien.* Amsterdam: Jan Wilting, 1656 AO, *Om Slaep te maecken*, pp. 57-58); Brau, Jean-Louis. *Historia de la droga* (orig. *Histoire de la drogue*). Barcelona: Bruguera, 1973, p. 76.

Figure 115. *Aguarda que te unten* (Wait till you've been anointed), *Los caprichos* (The Caprices), no. 67, aquatint and etching, Francisco Goya (1746 – 1828), Museo del Prado, Madrid.

A bridge between alchemy and iatrochemistry, Paracelsus was born in the year Columbus returned from his first voyage to the Indies "in a period of expansion, discovery, and rebellion."[40] His pharmacopeia "was a collection of arcana, magisteri, quintessences, and specifics, based mainly on the doctrines of alchemy and the cabalistic art."[41] A devoted alchemist, he sought and claimed to have discovered "the philosopher's stone, or tincture, which would have the power of producing gold."[42] Yet, he "denounced, in unmeasured terms, the accepted principles of medicine, as derived from the ancients,"[43] preferring to attack "the basic problem of the healing art, asking for the *how* and *why*. He was a scientist in search of a philosophy of medicine."[44]

Paracelsus advocated a therapy of *heroic* remedies.

His practice was of the heroic character. He discarded most of the milder and simpler remedies previously in vogue, and treated his patients with a variety of arcana, or specifics, extracted by alchemy from different mineral and organic bodies. Opium, a drug which no school of practitioner seems able to dispense with, was one of the few older remedies which he retained in his pharmacopeia.[45]

The heroic remedy is the consequence of a theory of pathology articulated about the idea of the organism as a totality, in which any kind of pain reveals the independence of one part of the body to the

---

[40] Sigerist, Henry E. Paracelsus in the Light of Four Hundred Years. NY: Columbia University Press, 1941 AO, p. 34.

[41] Dalton, J. C. Galen and Paracelsus. NY: D. Appleton and Company, 1873 AO, p. 28.

[42] Dalton (1873), p. 25.

[43] Dalton (1873), p. 18.

[44] Sigerist, Paracelsus (1941), p. 50.

[45] Dalton (1873), pp. 19-20.

detriment of the unity of the whole. Wrapped up in alchemical clothing, or veiled by contemporary casuistry, the method of Paracelsus is based upon certain drugs that displace to the outside the evil within. The entire organism had to be threatened with toxins specific to each illness so that its expulsion could provoke (in remediable cases) a *heroic* return to unity.[46] Paracelsus also discovered the nature of infection, thinking of sickness as something alive, which fed itself upon the life of the patient and which could be directly attacked with toxins. Faithful to the adage *that which sickens also cures*, he opened a fecund field of investigations employing mineral salts, mercury, zinc and all kinds of metals, combining the found with the strange but conscious of following a basically forward-looking orientation.

In his opinion, of all his remedies one of the most prodigious was opium. "The prescriptions [of Paracelsus] that contain opium, sucus, liquores or semen papaveris or oleum de papavere are innumerable."[47] We know, for example, the recipe for his *calming specific* (the anodyne) and it appears the work of a poet:

---

[46] Even in 1828 the philosopher George Wilhelm Frederich Hegel (1770 – 1831) explained disease, therapy and healing in much the same terms in his *Encyklopädie der Philosophischen Wissenschaften*. Leipzig: *Verlag der Bürrschen Buchhandlung*, 1870 AO, section 372, p. 323: *Die eigenthümliche Erscheinung der Krankheit ... der Versuch und Beginn der Heilung ist* (The peculiar appearance of the disease is, therefore, that the identity of the whole organic process manifests itself as the successive course of the movement of life through its different moments, sensitivity, irritability and reproduction; i.e., as fever, which, however, as the cause of totality against isolated activity, is just as much the attempt and the beginning of healing).

[47] Sigerist, Henry E. "Laudanum in the Works of Paracelsus," *Bulletin of the History of Medicine*, vol. 9, no. 5 (May 1941), Johns Hopkins University Press, AO, p. 540.

Take of Thebaic opium, one ounce; of orange and lemon juice, six ounces; of cinnamon and caryophylli, each half an ounce. Pound all these ingredients carefully together, mix them well, and place them in a glass vessel with its blind covering. Let them be digested in the sun or in dung for a month, and then afterwards pressed out and placed again in the vessel with the following: Half a scruple of musk, four scruples of ambergris, half an ounce of crocus, and one and a half scruple each of the juice of corals and of the magistery of pearls. Mix these, and, after digesting all for a month, add a scruple and a half of the quintessence of gold. When this is mixed with the rest it will be an anodyne specific, capable of removing any diseases, internal or external, so that no member of the body shall be further affected.[48]

And of all his preparations none possessed virtues as a heroic remedy comparable to laudanum, a tincture he invented which he always carried with him concealed in either the pommel of his saddle or the handle of his sword[49] during his extensive travels in "Germany, Italy, France, the Netherlands, Denmark, Sweden, and Russia .... It is [even] probable that Paracelsus stayed among the Tartars between 1513 and 1521."[50] Though he had little formal education, he visited various universities, "devoting himself in great measure to the study of alchemy and astrology, and practising the medical art wherever he happened to be."[51]

Sadly, his magisterial formula for laudanum is enveloped even today in clouds of smoke. Most investigators concur that it contained

---

[48] Waite, Arthur Edward, ed. The Hermetic and Alchemical Writings of Aureolus Philippus Theophrastus Bambast, of Hohenheim, called Paracelsus the Great, vol. II. London: James Elliott and Co., 1894 AO, Part II, Hermetic Medicine, The Archidoxies of Theophrastus Paracelsus, Book the Seventh, pp. 62-63.

[49] Stoddart, Anna M. The Life of Paracelsus. London: John Murray, 1911 AO, pp. 100-101.

[50] Hartmann, Franz. The Life and the Doctrines of Paracelsus. NY: Macoy Publishing and Masonic Supply Company, 1945 (1891) AO, pp. 5-6.

[51] Dalton (1873), p. 17.

gold leaf and unperforated pearls and some contend that its "chief ingredient"[52] was opium. But there is also argument that it "cannot possibly have any connection with opium. ... [T]here was no unanimity of opinion as to what the real laudanum Paracelsi actually had been."[53] What is true is that by the seventeenth century, laudanum "became a generic term for praiseworthy remedies, some of which contained opium, some not."[54]

Regardless of its composition, Paracelsus' laudanum earned its inventor extraordinary therapeutic success, allowing him to boast of saving the lives of many kings and princes. "He claimed to have cured no less than eighteen princes, of royal or ducal blood, who had previously found no benefit from the treatment of their regular physicians."[55] While extraordinary claims should rightly demand extraordinary evidence, there appears to be little doubt that he cured the great printer Frobenius of gangrene, thereby saving his right foot from amputation, and successfully treated the poor health of the

---

[52] Encyclopaedia Britannica, vol. XVI, L to Lord Advocate. Cambridge, UK: at the University Press, 1911 AO, "Laudanum," p. 278.

[53] Sigerist, "Laudanum" (1941), pp. 531, 544.

[54] Sigerist, "Laudanum" (1941), p. 544; a formula for laudanum (to be used only in desperate cases) in his collected works, for example, lists gold leaf, unperforated pearls, asphalt, flowers of antimony, oriental crocus, and Roman myrrh but no mention of opium (Paracelsi Bombast ab Hohenheim, Avr. Philip. Theoph. _Opera Omnia_, vol. I. Geneva: Sumptibus Ioan. Antonij, & Samuelis De Tournes, 1658 AO, p. 492, ch. XXI, _Libri quatuordecim Paragraphorum, Liber primus, cap. I, Paragraphvs V_: _Diffolutis ac deploratis ... Orizei foliati ... ad pondus omnium. Reduc ad formam. Dofis gr. vj.aut vij. vfque ad gr. x_); against this, Angelo Sala (1576 – 1637) in his _Opiologia_ (La Haye, NL: Chez Hillebrant Iacobffz, 1614 AO), for example, gives four separate recipes for laudanum containing opium in chapter eight (pp. 33 – 42).

[55] Dalton (1873), p. 18.

renowned humanist Erasmus of Rotterdam, whose correspondence on this matter with Paracelsus survives.[56]

In 1526 at the age of thirty-three, his celebrity led the Town Council of Basel to offer him the position of municipal physician, making him also a Professor of Medicine and Surgery at the University.[57] There, his unorthodox views and quarrelsome, self-assertive personality excited a violent opposition (who nicknamed him *Cacaphrastus*)[58] and within two years he was gone. One of his last resonating successes was to cure the gout of an eminent ecclesiastic, Canonicus Cornelius of Lichtenfels,[59] who then refused to pay all that he had promised. Paracelsus sued, lost and then, unwisely, "assailed the judge with vituperation, and was obliged to leave Basle"[60] in the dead of night. He left behind him, in this city and in its university, the foundations of pharmaceutical chemistry and with it a noteworthy impetus to this occupation as an industry.

His absence was enough to demonstrate that he possessed a multitude of followers, not only among cured patients but also in the medical estate. Among the latter were the Swiss physician and specialist in psychiatric diseases Felix Platter (Plater, 1536 – 1614) and the physician and naturalist Conrad Gessner (1516 – 1565), sometimes called the Swiss Pliny for his four volume *Historia animalium*. Developing the Paracelsian orientation, they demolished the Galenic criterion that classified opium as a toxin cold in the fourth degree and the solanaceas psychoactive in the third.[61] Although by then there was

---

[56] Sigerist, Paracelsus (1941), p. 42.

[57] Sigerist, Paracelsus (1941), p. 42; Dalton (1873), p. 18.

[58] Stoddart (1911), p. vii; Dalton (1873), p. 22.

[59] Hartmann (1945), p. 9; Dalton (1873), p. 22.

[60] Dalton (1873), p. 22; Stoddart (1911), p. 138.

[61] "Both Dioscorides and Galen had written that opium had a strongly cooling and drying effect [but] some medical authors, such as ... Felix Platter ... had attributed a

a revival in Europe of the triacal tradition, this traditional use will not have a future so much as a substance used alone as it will in preparations oriented toward a particular efficacy. It began to be administered in large doses for a wide range of functions including as an anaesthetic in surgery.[62]

Not long after Paracelsus' death, laudanum prepared by the Abbot Rousseau[63] is the daily drug of Cardinal Armand Jean du Plessis de Richelieu (1585 – 1642) and Louis XIV (1638 – 1715), as well as the constant counsel of the celebrated French poet Pierre de Ronsard (1524 – 1585).[64] It was the *scientific* drug *par excelence*, whose handling

---

warm quality to opium" (Klerk, Saskia. "The Trouble with Opium," *Early Science and Medicine* 19 (2014), Brill, academia.edu, p. 309).

[62] One recipe for the laudanum of Paracelsus contained among other things, "Opium Thebaick ... Juice of Henbane, in due time gathered, and first thickened in the Sun ... Salt of Pearls ... Corals ... Unicorns-horn ... Anise, Carroways, Oranges, Citrons, Nutmegs, Cloves, Cinnamon, [and] Amber. ... [T]he Oyles ... which, afterward being fermented by digestion ... set in the most gentle heat of Ashes, are rendrost of greater efficacy and operation (Hartman, John, tr. Bazilica Chymica, & Praxis Chymiatricae OR Royal and Practical Chymistry, a translation of Oswald Crollius' Royal Chymistry. London: John Starkey and Thomas Passinger, 1670 quod.lib.umich.edu, chapter VII Anodynes, pp. 87 – 89); Sala in *Opiologia* (1614), gives twenty-four different classes of ailments that can benefit from the use of laudanum containing opium including surgical amputation (p. 53) in chapter nine (pp. 42 – 55).

[63] Rousseau, Abbé. *Secrets et Remedes Eprovez*, second edition. Paris: Chez Claude Jombert, 1718 AO, Premiere Partie, Chapitre 11, p. 75: *On applique fagement une doze convenable de Laudanum bien préparé, & à l'inftant le calme vient comme par un miracle* (One applies wisely an appropriate dose of well-prepared Laudanum, and instantly calm comes like a miracle).

[64] Ronsard, Pierre de. *Oeuvres Completes de P. de Ronsard*, vol. 8, ed. Paul Laumonier. Paris: Librarie Alphonse Lemerre, 1919 AO, "*Notice Biographique sur Pierre de Ronsard*," p. 262: *Les insomnies étaient son plus cruel supplice. ... le pavot ... ne lui causait qu'une sorte d'abattement, qu'il décrit dans un sonnet où il porte envie aux animaux hibernantes: Heureux, cent fois heureux, animaux qui dormez ... Sans manger du pauot qui tous les ſens aſſomme: l'en ay*

and prescription separated the serious faculty from the apprentices and *curanderos*. At times the Inquisition did not recognize this difference and persecuted its proponents, as happened with Porta, though this reaction is isolated and occasional. However, the same did not happen in the later tribunals of the Protestant world, which recognized the consolidation of pharmaceutical chemistry as a discipline and as a commercial enterprise, already flourishing in Switzerland and Germany.

But the impulse that drove Paracelsus and his disciples to the rediscovery of opium was also connected to the rise of Genoa and Venice as the first naval powers in the Mediterranean, which allowed them to receive without complications the Theban product, many times prepared in the form of triacas. From 1442 there began to arrive ships filled with the substance from the sultanate of Egypt, and a little while later Venice became a manufacturer and exporter of the *triaca magna* or *galenica*, manufactured with great solemnity, following rites fixed more than a millennium earlier by the Roman emperor Antoninus Pius.[65] One of the reasons for this active commerce from Alexandria to European ports is the devaluation of the historical silk route, the only traditional road between the Middle and the Far East, due to the instability of the difficult passes and deserts of the Persian zone, as well as to the fall of the Mameluke Empire and the cheaper maritime transport by the Cape of Good Hope; these circumstances caused opium production to flow toward the Mediterranean from the area today covered by Egypt, Turkey and Iran.

After a practically absolute obscurity during the first Christian millennium, the traditional drug of the Mediterranean basin reappears now as a great novelty. It comes via the hands of alchemists and

---

mangé, i'ai beu de ſon iuſt oublieux ... (citing vol. VI, pp. 4, 7).
[65] Aparicio, 1972, p. 169.

CH. 12 CHRISTIANITY AND EBRIETY (III)

Hippocratic physicians and emerges as the emblem of incipient iatrochemistry. This happens right when doctors trained in universities are attacking medieval and domestic remedies as coarse things, of little practical use and covered in superstition.

The therapeutic class continues centuries consolidating itself, and by 1518 King Henry VIII charters the Royal College of Physicians in London, to which the Crown granted the privilege of handing out licenses for the treatment of all kinds of patients in the city and its environs. Faced with the drugs of the Celtic culture and with alcohol, the physicians with university diplomas demonstrated to their clients their professional superiority by prescribing opiate compounds, with infallible effects for various symptoms. Opium symbolizes modernity and curative virtues, while increasing the social depreciation of the old drugs, as well as the new, tobacco and coffee.

It is in this climate when the oldest pharmacopeias in Europe were published. The German physician and naturalist Valerius Cordús (1515 – 1544) compiles the first in Nuremberg, published two years after his death as the _Dispensatorivm Pharmacorvm_ in 1546. Anuces Foës (Anvtio Foesio, 1528 – 1595) records the first use of the term in his _Pharmacopoeia Medicamentorvm_, published in Basel in 1561.[66] Both were profoundly influenced by the idea of the heroic. The solanaceas appear as valid agents always when they are combined with opium, and it is certainly curious that there will be "so scarce a difference between the composition on the one hand of analgesics and soporifics and on the other the preparations of the witches."[67]

In the _Labyrinthus Medicorum_, Paracelsus writes that the job of the alchemist was to separate the pure from the impure:

---

[66] Holmes, Edward Morel. "Pharmacopoeia," The Encyclopaedia Britannica, vol. 21, eleventh edition. Cambridge, UK: at the University Press, 1911 AO, p. 353.
[67] Brau, 1973, p. 76.

Anyone who would become a physician must learn the book of Alchemy thoroughly by heart. ... Alchemy is an Art, and Vulcan is the operator therein. ... Know, then, that this only is Alchemy, which, by preparation through fire, separates what is impure, and draws out the pure. ... Bread is created and given to us by God, but not in the shape which the baker confers upon it. Those three Vulcans, the farmer, the miller, and the baker, produce from that first matter a second, bread. The same should be done with medicaments ....[68]

The road opening up now is the purification of the most active substances, which already points toward the later discoveries of their principal chemical constituents, the alkaloids. But the immediate metamorphosis was to accomplish the transformation to scientific pharmacology, an occupation that secularly was midway between alchemy and open witchcraft, two activities persecuted by Christian orthodoxy. Initially, it was enough to change the cauldron for the retort, the unguent for the tablet.

B.   The State of Things in the Americas

That the treasure of the Americas was basically botanical never entered into the calculations of the conquistadors, though they quickly adapted to it. Hernán Cortés de Monroy y Pizarro Altamirano (1485 – 1547) noted the variety of these new plants and medicines in the capital city of Motezuma: "There is also an herb street, where may be obtained all sorts of roots and medicinal herbs that the country affords. There are apothecaries' shops, where prepared medicines, liquids, ointments, and plasters are sold."[69]

---

[68] Waite, The Hermetic and Alchemical Writings, vol. II (1894), pp. 165, 167.
[69] Folsom, George, tr. The Despatches of Hernando Cortes. NY: Wiley and Putnam, 1843 AO, Letter II, chapter V, p. 112.

Figure 116. *Hechiceros de sueños* (Sorcerers of Dreams), Felipe Guaman Poma de Ayala. *Nueva Corónica y Buen Gobierno*. Caracas: Biblioteca Ayacucho, 1980 AO, p. 196.

The Tlaxcaltecas cured Cortés of a wound in the head with great skill after his retreat from Tenochtitlan.[70]

They added, that since I had returned wounded, and all my company were worn down with toil, we should go to a city four leagues from this town, where we might obtain repose, and they would strive to cure our wounds and recover us from the effects of our fatigue and exhaustion.[71]

He was not alone in his praise of the healing arts found there:

They have their doctors, with natural experience, who know how to apply many herbs and medicines, which for them is enough; and there are some of them with such experience that many old and grave illnesses, which the Spaniards had suffered long days without finding a remedy, those Indians cured them. In that city of Tlaxcallan there was in the year 1537 an imposing hospital ....[72]

Some of the Spaniards preferred this new medicine:

The empirical medicine of the aborigines, throughout the Americas, knew many [therapeutic plants] and employed them with such success that there was a time when the conquistadores preferred the empiricism of the indigenous *curanderos* to the science of the European doctors.[73]

---

[70] *En esta provincia de Tascaltecal estuve veinte días curándome de las heridas que traía* ... (Cortés, Hernán. *Cartas de Relación de la Conquista de Méjico*, vol. I. Madrid: Calpe, 1922 AO, Carta Segunda, p. 148); "On this occasion I was badly wounded in the head by two stones .... I remained in this province of Tascaltecal twenty days, for the purpose of healing my wounds ..." (Folsom, Despatches, Letter II, chapter VII, pp. 164, 169); Diaz del Castillo, Capitan Bernal. *Historia Verdadera de la Conquista de la Nueva España*, vol. II. Paris: Libreria de Rosa, 1837 AO, ch. cxxviii, pp. 346-347.

[71] Folsom, Despatches, Letter II, chapter VII, p. 167.

[72] Motolinia, Toribio de Benavente o. *Historia de los Indios de la Nueva España*. Barcelona: Herederos de Juan Gili, Editores, 1914 BHO, p. 131.

[73] Lamas, Andrés. *Introduccion*, in Lozano, Pedro. *Historia de la Conquista del Paraguay*,

In 1637 one of the first rectors of the University of Lima, Peru, the philologue Dr. Alonso de Huerta (1556? – 1650) who had learned Quechua, opposed financing a Cathedral of Medicine there "because in this kingdom there are many medicinal herbs for many illnesses and wounds which the Indians know better than the physicians and with them they cure without having need of doctors."[74]

Instead of going to the Americas to substitute for the local therapists, many botanists and Spanish physicians sailed there to be instructed trying, as the historian Bernardo de Vargas Machuca (1555? – 1622) explained, to learn these plants "some known by the Indians, how such great herbalists and others acquired it with experience, how each one would do it, discovering new medicines ...."[75] The admiration and genuine scientific curiosity crystallized in the work of the naturalist and court physician to King Philip II, Francisco Hernández de Toledo (1514? – 1587), who spent seven years traveling in the new world and catalogued over 3000 different plants (the _Materia medica_ of Dioscorides discussed some three hundred), which permitted Europe to know in detail the richness of the American flora and to be amazed by it.[76]

---

vol. I, ed. Andrés Lamas. Buenos Aires: Casa Editora Imprenta Popular, 1873 AO, pp. lxxvi – lxxv: _La medicina empírica de los aborígenes ... de los médicos europeos._

[74] Perez de Barradas, J. _Plantas Magicas Americanas._ Madrid: CSIC, 1957, p. 23; Lamas, in Lozano (1873), _Introduccion_, p. LXXV: _no ser necesarias; porque en este reino hay muchas yerbas medicinales para muchas enfermedades y heridas; las cuales conocen los indios mejor que los medicos, y con ellas se curan sin haber menester medicos_ (citing Libro 4 de _Claustros_, p. 185); _se negó categóricamente ... los estudios de Medicina en la Universidad limeña, aduciendo que los prácticas sanitarias incas eran mucho mas efectivas_ (Biblioteca Virtual de la Filología Española, bvfe.es).

[75] _[A]lgunos sabidas de los indios, como tan grandes herbolarios ... descubriendo nuevos medicamentos_ (Vargas Machuca, Bernardo de. _Milicia y Descripción de las Indias_, vol. I. Madrid: Librería de Victoriano Suarez, 1892 (1599) AO, pp. 139-140).

[76] Protomedico for all the New World, from 1570 to 1580 Hernández wrote the _Historia Natural de las Indias_ which was composed of 17 thick illustrated (by

Apart from that, they had good reason to be astonished. The Aztec culture, so barbarous in other respects, possessed sumptuous botanical gardens which were at the same time places of recreation for the court, pharmacological storehouses and investigative laboratories. The dramatist and historian Antonio de Solís y Ribadeneyra (1610 – 1686) described the botanical gardens of Motezuma:

They had herbs for all Kinds of Pains and Infirmities; and in the Juices and Application of thefe Herbs confifted all their Remedies, and with thefe they effected furprizing Cures ... applying them to the Patient's great Benefit and Recovery. The King freely diftributed to all who had Occafion for them fuch of his Simples as were prefcrib'd by the Phyficians, or defir'd by the Sick; and was wont to inquire if the Patient had received any Benefit therefrom, either gratifying a fort of Vanity he had in the Fuccefsful Operation of his Medicines, or believing that he fulfill'd the Obligation of a Sovereign, in taking fuch care of the Health of his Vaffals.[77]

In Mexico the *ticitl* (healer, physician, midwife) were often family castes, like the Greek Asclepians.[78] The apothecaries (*papiani*) sold their remedies in the markets, though the needy could obtain their medicines at no cost from the botanical gardens.[79] According to the

---

indigenous Indians almost always) volumes. The original copy, kept in the library at El Escorial, was lost due to a fire on 17 July 1671, though there remained an extensive compendium, published in Italy under the title _Rervm Medicarvm Novae Hispaniae Thesavrus_, ed. A Nardo Antonio Reechi. Romae: Ex Typgrapheio Vitalis Mascardi, 1651 AO.

[77] Solis, Antonio de. The History of the Conquest of Mexico by the Spaniards, vol. I, tr. Thomas Townsend, ed. Nathaniel Hooke. London: Printed for John Osborn, 1738 BHO, book III, ch. XIV, *Of the different Pleafure-Houfes which Motezuma had for his Recreation*, pp. 407-408; Caro Baroja, _Las brujas_, 1966, p. 162.

[78] Molina, Alonfo de. _Vocabvlario en lengva castellana y mexicana_. En Mexico: En Cafa de Antonio de Spinofa, 1571 BHO, part two, f. 113r

[79] Molina (1571), part two, f. 80r.

CH. 12 CHRISTIANITY AND EBRIETY (III)

Franciscan missionary Toribio de Benavente (d. 1568), nicknamed Motolinia (poor) by the Indians because of his rags, they also had a number of great hospitals, well provisioned for the sick and indigent.[80]

However, the admiration and the desire to learn soon ran up against an obstacle greater than racial prejudice and other ethnocentric clichés. Many of these medicinal drugs were psychoactive, and not a few were employed in religious or analogous contexts. Following directives that were then all the rage in Europe, the clergy and soldiers understood that these initial pharmacolcial studies had to be combined with an exhaustive Inquisitional inquiry. Upon exploring the zone of Darien, the conquistador and eyewitness to the conquest of the isthmus of Panama, Pascual de Andagoya (1495 – 1548) encountered

sorcerers and witches who did much harm to children, and even to grown up people, at the suggestion of the devil, who gave them his salves, with which they anointed those whom they bewitched. These salves were made from certain herbs. On inquiring in what form the devil appeared, it was stated that he took the form of a beautiful boy, in order that the people, being simple, might not be terrified, and might believe him. ... These and many other things are contained in the information which I received from the witches themselves, who said they anointed people with the salves which were given to them by the enemy.[81]

---

[80] *Han hecho los Indios muchos hospitales adonde curan los enfermos y pobres ... que los hospitales están bien proveídos ...* (Benavente o Motolinia, *Historia*, 1914, p. 131).

[81] Andragoya, Pascual de. <u>Narrative of the Proceeding of Pedrarius Davila</u>, tr. Clements R. Markham. London: Printed for the Hakluyt Society, 1865 AO, p. 14; Caro Baroja, 1966, p. 162; *En estas provincias habia brujas y brujos ... y que se untaban con la uncion que les daba el enemigo ...* (Navarette, Martin Fernández de. <u>*Coleccion de los viajes y descubrimiento*</u>, vol. III. Madrid: En la Imprenta Real, 1829 AO, Seccion III. *Establicimientos de los Españoles en el Darien*, no. VII, *Relacion de los sucesos de Pedrarias Dávila*, p. 400).

There was in reality no way to distinguish with any clarity the eminent doctors and indigenous drugmakers from the infernal wizards. What some considered marvelous cures were for others something magical, deserving to be purified by fire. While Hernán Cortés was cured of his wounds by indigenous healers and the Rector of the University of Lima begged European doctors *not* be sent to the Americas, others demanded protection for the poor children stewed by the witches and for the innocent victims of diabolic evil.

Moreover, in the opinion of the crusaders a reciprocal current of feeding between the Old and New Worlds had been established. Thanks to the Holy Office and the Protestant tribunals many European witches emigrated on their broomsticks to other continents, and thanks to the efforts of the missionaries many American and Asiatic shamans fled to Europe in the same way. Consequently, the oceans saw themselves crossed in all directions by flying apostates.

Pierre Rosteguy De Lancre (1553 – 1631), one of the royal judges appointed by Henry IV of France to deal with sorcerers and witches in the Labourd region of Bordeaux at the beginning of the seventeenth century, wrote a book using the case files from his investigations:

But his explanation of the growing forces of evil in his time soon becomes a truly fantastic hodge-podge of religion, politics and political geography. He [De Lancre] speaks of the emigration of devils from America, Japan and other parts where missionary work had been successful, for instance, and claims that the outcasts had settled happily in the much neglected Labourd region, winning over the souls of women, children and even priests. He was able to assure his readers that a number of English and Scottish travellers who had come to Bordeaux by sea had actually seen great hordes of devils making for France – doubtless in search of more living space, and better accomodation.[82]

---

[82] De Lancre, Pierre. *Tableuv de L'inconstance des Mavvais Anges et Demons*. Paris: Chez

CH. 12 CHRISTIANITY AND EBRIETY (III)

Famous for his bloodthirst within a line of the bloodthirsty (including among the other French theorists of the crime of witchcraft the aforementioned Jean Bodin, the Burgundian judge Henry Boquet (1550 – 1619),[83] and the magistrate Nicolas Remy (1530 – 1616), who supposedly had executed over 800 suspects),[84] De Lancre seeded in the lands of Lombardy a terror based on the same reasoning of the American missionaries: the demons have a relationship with diabolic herbs and when they enter a person the best for them (as for everyone) consists in giving them relief by torture ending in the bonfire.

In the Americas there will be some indecision between recognizing indigenous wisdom and accepting Christian theology, between taking advantage of the rich medicinal flora and suppressing any temptation to apostasy. These vacillations appear to be expressed in a transparent manner in a work published by the physician Juan de Cárdenas (1563 – 1609) in 1591, whose last chapter talks about the

---

Iean Berjon, 1612 BNF, Livre I, Discouvrs II, pp. 39-40: *Qui me fait croire que la ceuotion ... grandes troupes de Demons en forme d'hommes efprouuentables paffer en France*; Caro Baroja, World, 1971, p. 159.

[83] Boquet convicts with nothing more than an anecdotal story of lost keys and cats who became wives: *Discovrs Execrable des Sorciers*. Paris: Chez Denis Binet, 1603 BNF, ch. 46 *De la metamorphofe*, p. 114; Caro Baroja, World, 1971, pp. 118, 283 ft 17.

[84] "Drawn from the capital trials of 900 persons, more or less, who within the last fifteen years have in Lorraine paid the penalty of death for the crime of witchcraft" (Remy, Nicolas. Demonolatry, tr. E. A. Ashwin, ed. Montague Summers. London: John Rodker, 1930 AO, title page); Remigii, Nicolai. *Daemonolatreiae Libri Tres*. Coloniae: Apud Henricum Falckenburg, 1596 AO: *Ex ivdiciis capitalibvs nongentorum plus minus hominum, qui fortilegij crimen intra annos quindecimi in Lotharingia capite luerunt*; the claim may have been little more than hype to sell books.

hechizos en las yervas (the witchery of herbs).[85] In line with the humanists, Cárdenas begins by affirming that

I thought it necessary to explain to the common people what everybody calls spells and enchantment really is, because every day I hear two thousand accounts, stories and fairy-tales about it. [...] We should seriously doubt this, and explain how herbs can operate naturally in our bodies without the intervention of a pact with the devil or a miracle ....[86]

The declaration appears to be Greek or Roman, and expresses the basis of the Hippocratic school. But Cárdenas did not wish to risk his luck like Porta, and perhaps even felt at heart the principles of the crusade. So a little later he states that "it is right to verify now if there is some herb or root in nature whose virtue should be so effective or powerful that through it we can force the devil to come at our call or by it we can divine some future event."[87]

The question occupies some paragraphs, in which medicinal laicism debates with Christian piety, until achieving a compromise

---

[85] *En que se declara muy por entero si puede aver lechizos en las yervas, y que sean hechizos* (Cárdenas, Iuan de. *Primera Parte de los Problemas y Secretos Marauillosos de las Indias*. En Mexico: Casa de Pedro Ocharte, 1591 AO, capítulo vltimo, p. 208).

[86] Pardo-Tomás, José. "Natural knowledge and medical remedies in the book of secrets: uses and appropriations in Juan de Cárdenas' *Problemas y secretos maravillosos de las Indias* (Mexico, 1591)," [Barcelona: CSIC] in Passion for Plants: Materia Medica and Botany in Scientific Networks from the 16th to 18th centuries, ed. Sabine Anagnostou et al. Stuttgart: Wissanschafliche Verlagsgesellschaft mbH, 2011 academia.edu, p. 104; *me parecio declarar, y dar a entender al vulgo, que sea esto que comunmente llaman todos hechizos, y enhechizar ... lo que las yervas pueden hazer, y obrar en nuestros cuerpos naturalmente, sin intervenir pacto con el demonio, o por ventura negocio de milagro ...* (Cárdenas, 1591, p. 208).

[87] *es justo averiguar agora si alguna yerva or rays aya en la naturaleza ... adevinemos alguna cosa por venir* (Cárdenas, 1591, p. 215).

solution. The well-intentioned will use these herbs (specifically speaking of *Peyot, del Poyomate, del hololifque, y aun del Piciete* (peyote, poyomatli, ololiuhqui, and even tobacco)[88] in agreement with their medicinal virtues, and the others will use them for apostate ends. There is not, then, a cultural use and a superstitious use, but only a worthy use and a punishable use.

Prefiguring completely the present-day distinction, Cárdenas maintains that the same drug, in the same dose and assimilated by the same person can possess diametrically opposite effects:

The man that uses the above-mentioned herbs for a good end, I want to say, for the purpose of curing some illness, because also these herbs are very medicinal ... will not see the Devil come nor know things to come; the contrary occurs with one who uses such herbs for a bad end ... to see the Devil and know things that are not known ... and would be better not to know.[89]

It is worth noting that Cárdenas attributes to agents of this kind the visionary trances of European antiquity: "Also when we read or hear it said that the Sibyls, and the priests of Apollo, Jupiter and Diana went mad when they wanted to give the answers of their gods, it must be that they were driven mad with some strong herb like these."[90] In reality, this evaluation of apostasy is made against many of the persons persecuted and tried for consuming or officiating with these traditional drugs.

In 1629 for example the Inquisitor Hernando Ruiz de Alarcón y Mendoza (17th c.) launched a crusade against the natives of Morelos

---

[88] *el Hombre que usa de las sobredichas yervas a buen fin ... les estaría mejor no saber* (Cárdenas, 1591, p. 215).
[89] Cárdenas, 1591, pp. 217-218.
[90] Cárdenas, 1591, p. 217.

and Guerrero, because they used psychotropic plants to enter into a trance in order to reveal the cause of their illness, and

> they attribute it all to the divinity of *ololiuhqui* or peyote, for which for this reason they have so much veneration and fear that they do however much they can [to conceal it], and they withdraw so that it will not come to the notice of the ecclesiastical ministers, especially if they are judges who can prohibit and punish it.[91]

There followed public burnings of the seeds, exfoliation of the fields, trials and condemnations. Well into the eighteenth century (when the European churches preferred to draw a thick veil over the crusade against the witches) we find inquisitorial trials against American herbalists. Even fully into the nineteenth century, various historians continued to present a conception of the Nahuatl and Mayan worlds as "a secret organization opposed to Christianity and the government."[92]

1.   Tobacco.   From the Mississippi valley to Tierra del Fuego, every American drank, ate or smoked this herb (*Nicotiana tabacum*), one of the most sacred of either continent. On the fifth island he encountered, *Juana* [Cuba], Cristóbal Colón (1447? – 1506) sent out two Spaniards, Rodrigo de Jerez and Luis de Torres, to

---

[91] Ruiz de Alarcón, Hernando. Treatise on the Heathen Superstitions, tr. J. Richard Andrews and Ross Hassig. Norman, OK: University of Oklahoma Press, 1984 GB, ch. 6, About the Superstition Concerning *Ololiuhqui*, p. 60; *porque todo lo atribuyen a la diuinidad ... los ministros eclesiasticos ...* (Ruiz de Alarcón, Hernando. *Tratado de las supersticiones y costumbres gentilicas que hoy viven entre los indios naturales de esta Nueva España*. Mexico, D. F.: Fuente Cultural, 1953 cervantesvirtual.com, *tratado premiere*, cap. VI, De la supersticion del ololiuhqui, para 97).

[92] *La idea del nagualismo como una peligrosa secta ... una organización secret que pretendía oponerse al cristianismo y al gobierno* (Garza, Mercedes de la. *Sueno y alucinacion en el mundo nahuatl y maya*. Mexico, DF: Instituto de Investigaciones Filogicas, UNAM, 1990 doku.pub, pp. 145-146).

examine the place. They became the first Europeans to follow the Indians in their custom of smoking cylinders of tobacco leaves:

Friday 2 November. The Admiral decided to send out two Spaniards, one called Rodrigo de Jerez who lived in Ayamonte, and the other a certain Luis de Torres who had lived with the Adelantado de Murcia and had been a Jew and, he says, knew Hebrew and Chaldean and some Arabic, and with them two Indians, one from among those he had brought from Guanahannd [sic]. ... Tuesday 6 November. The two Christians found many people, men and women, on their journey who were on their way to their villages carry a smouldering brand of herbs which they are accustomed to smoke.[93]

De Jerez returned to Spain where he continued smoking until imprisoned by the Inquisition for seven years because [supposedly] "only Satan could confer on a man the faculty of expelling smoke from the mouth."[94]

The Bishop of Chiapas, Bartolomé de las Casas (1474 – 1566), tells much the same story regarding the two Spaniards and the indigenous custom of smoking what he calls small muskets:

---

[93] The Diary of Christopher Columbus, Research at King's College London, Early Modern Spain, Diary of 1492, ems.kcl.ac.uk; *Viernes 2 de noviembre. Acordó el Almirante enbiar dos hombres españoles ... con un tizóu en la mano, yervas para tomar sus sahumerios que acostumbravan* (*Diario*, ems.kcl.ac.uk); Major, R. H., tr., ed. Select Letters of Christopher Columbus. London: Printed for the Hakluyt Society, 1870 AO, First Voyage of Columbus, A Letter sent by Columbus to [Luis de Santangel] Chancellor of he Exchequer [of Aragon], p. 3: *enbie dos hombres por la tierra para saber si auia rey o grandes ciudades* [I sent two men ashore to ascertain whether there was any king or large cities in that part].

[94] Perez de Barradas, 1957, p. 46.

Figure 117. *Nicotiana tabacum*, tobacco plant.

CH. 12 CHRISTIANITY AND EBRIETY (III)

[They found] men with half-burned wood in their hands and certain herbs to take their smokes, which are some dry herbs put in a certain leaf, also dry, like those the boys make on the day of the Passover of the Holy Ghost; and having lighted one part of it, by the other they suck, absorb, or receive that smoke inside with the breath, by which they become benumbed and almost drunk, and so it is said they do not feel fatigue. These muskets as we will call them, they call *tabacos.*[95]

De las Casas added that this *barbarous* practice was rapidly being disseminated among his compatriots. He was also one of the first to perceive the intense addictivity of the new substance, as many reported they lacked the *power to refrain*: "I knew Spaniards on this island of Española who were accustomed to take it, and being reprimanded for it, by telling them it was a vice, they replied they were unable to cease using it. I do not know what relish or benefit they found in it."[96]

The Spanish historian, botanist and ethnographer Gonzalo Fernández de Oviedo y Valdés (1478 – 1557), the oldest chronicler of the Indies, wrote a picturesque tale of its effects, comparing it to henbane:

The Indians use in this island among their other vices one very bad one, which is to take some smoked leaves, that they call *tabaco*, to go out of their senses. And this they do with the smoke of a certain herb which, as I have been given to understand,

---

[95] Hodge, Frederick Webb, ed. Handbook of American Indians North of Mexico, part 2. Washington, DC: Government Printing Office, 1910 AO, Tobacco, p. 767; *los hombres con un tizon en las manos, y ciertas hierbas para tomar sus sahumerios ... con el cual se adormecen las carnes y cuasi emborracha, y así, diz que, no sienen el cansancio. Estos mosquetes, ó como los llamaremos, llaman ellos tabacos* (Casas, Fray Bartolomé de las. *Historia de las Indias*, ed. Augustín Millares Carlo, vol. I. Mexico, DF: Fondo de Cultura Economica, 1951 AO, cap. XLVI, pp. 230-231); Lewin, 1964, pp. 287-288.
[96] Hodge, 1910, p. 767; *Españoles cognoscí yo en esta isla Española ... respondian que no era en su mano dejarlos de tomar; no se qué sabor ó provecho hallaban en ellos* (Casas, 1951, p. 231); Lewin, 1964, p. 288.

775

is a kind of henbane. ... I know that some Christians already use it ... because they say that those who take it ... and are thus transported do not feel the pains of their illness, and it does not appear to me that this is anything other than death in life.[97]

The similarity between henbane and tobacco (both of course are solanaceas) is not only based on the notable psychoactivity of the latter in its first administrations, but also in the ritual use which characterized and still characterizes the use of tobacco in certain areas. For example, in the eastern jungles of Peru and Ecuador the Jibaro shamans initiate young men into the *arutam* cult:

Often, an older, experienced warrior accompanies a small band of youths as they undertake a trek of several days far into the forest. ... The eminent warrior presides. Tobacco is smoked or masticated; juice squeezed from the bark of *maikua* (*Datura arborea*) is imbibed. In a visionary ordeal, the initiate must withstand the violent effects of the hallucinogen ....[98]

Besides the groups that used the drugs in more profane contexts, many also used them for therapeutic ends. Fray Ramón Pané (15th c. – 16th c.), whose ethnological study of the Tainos became the first book published in the Americas in a European language, recorded its medicinal use as a purgative within a larger spiritual context reminiscent of the rites of the Asclepians:

---

[97] *Usaban los indios desta isla ... estar muerto en vida* (Oviedo y Valdés, Gonzalo Fernandez de. *Historia general y natural de las indias*, primera parte, ed. José Amador de los Rios. Madrid: Imprenta de la Real Academia de la Historia, 1851 AO, libro V, ch. 2, *De los tabacos*, pp. 130-131). The similarity to the effects of henbane could be due to other habitual ingredients being used then, as cohoba or yopo (*Anadenanthera peregrina*), a source of dimethyltryptamine (DMT).

[98] Kelekna, Pita. "Farming, Feuding, and Female Status: the Achuar Case," in Amazonian Indians from Prehistory to Present: Anthropological Perspectives, ed. Anna Roosevelt. Tucson, AZ: University of Arizona Press, 1994, pp.240-241.

CH. 12 CHRISTIANITY AND EBRIETY (III)

The doctor [*behique*] ... in order to purge [the patient] takes a certain powder, called cohoba, breathing it in through the nose, which makes them drunk in such a way that they don't know what they are doing; and in this way they say many things outside of judgment, during which they affirm that they speak with the *cemies*, and that those tell them from whence came the infirmity.[99]

Otherwise, the accounts of both Las Casas and Oviedo coincide in that inhaling the smoke provoked somnolence and intoxication, although *manifestly* it blocked the Indians from feeling fatigue. Neither of the two appears to have had any trouble with the paradox of a drug that induces sleep and relieves pain at the same time. It is of course true that tobacco can act as both a sedative and a stimulant. In spite of what happened with Rodrigo de Jerez and Luis de Torres, the criticism of Las Casas and the commentary of Oviedo, there are not in the Americas indications of an overly intense inquisitional persecution connected with this drug, very probably due to its rapid success among the invaders.

Many European countries set up monopolies to import and tax the new drug. Spain got out front when Philip III (1578 – 1621) decreed in 1614 that all tobacco would be imported solely through the *Casa de Contratación* [House of Trade] in Sevilla. By 1632 the legislative assembly was taxing salt fish, chocolate and tobacco.[100] In England James I (1566 – 1625) in his <u>A Covnter-blaste to Tobacco</u> (1604)

---

[99] Pané, Ramón. <u>*Relación Acerca de las Antigüedades de los Indios*</u>, ed. Josē Juan Arrom. Madrid: Siglo Veintiuno, 1968, ch. XV, *De las observaciones de estos indios behiques*, p. 35: *Cuando alguno está enfermo, le llevan el behique, que es el médico sobredicho. ... y que éstos les dicen que de ellos les han venido la enfermedad.*

[100] *Que por quanto el Reyno junto en cortes, en las del año de mil y feifciétos y treinta y dos ... que fon los impuestos en ... tabaco* (<u>*Escritvras, Acverdos, Administraciones, y Svplicas*</u>. Madrid: Por Diego Diaz de la Carrera, 1659 (GB), *Escritvra del servicio de los dos millones, y medio, f. 104*).

famously called it a "custome lothsome to the eye, hateful to the Nose, harmefull to the braine, dangerous to the Lungs, and in the blacke stinking fume thereof, neerest resembling the horrible Stigian smoke of the pit that is bottomelesse."[101] He then proclaimed a heavy tax to try to discourage imports from Spain.[102] Twenty years later, after the North American product became popular, he dissolved the charter of the Virginia Company and established a crown monopoly on the drug.

2.   Coca.   In order of importance by the quantity of declared consumers, the second great drug discovered in the Americas was the coca leaf (*Erythroxylon coca*). As we have seen, the cultivation of this plant was ubiquitous throughout the Incan Empire, which to the Spanish seemed in the beginning to be contemptible. This hostility (and the general depravation and disease brought by the conquistadors) caused the coca fields in some regions to be abandoned and the popularity of the drug to initially decrease. Even so, according to the earliest chronicler of Peru, Pedro de Cieza de León (1518 – 1560), it continued to be valuable and allowed some Spaniards to amass fortunes buying and reselling it in the markets as well as in the mines of Potosí.[103]

At the same time, however, successive Councils (1551 – 1552 and 1567 – 1568) expressly denounced the use of the leaf as an

---

[101] James VI and I. A Royal Rhetorician, ed. Robert S. Rait. Westminster: A Constable and Co., 1900 AO, p. 54.

[102] James VI and I, 1900, p. 59.

[103] *Esta coca se llevaba a vender a las minas de Potosí ... Algunos están en España ricos ... rescatándola en los tiangues o mercados a los indios* (De León, Pedro de Cieza. *La Crónica del Perú*, part one. Madrid: Calpe, 1922 AO, cap. XCVI, *Cómo en todas las más de las Indies usaron ... la preciada hierba llamada coca*, p. 305); Lewin, 1964, p. 76.

idolatrous practice at the same time that a proclamation of the Viceroy stated that its effects were the product of a diabolic illusion.[104]

As early as 1552, the prelates who gathered for the First Council of Lima were informed of its use in divination and pagan sacrifices. They were advised to dissuade the neophytes from making offerings to the sun, earth, and sea with coca, maize, water, or any other thing. The more vehement coca opponents were convinced that coca was the invention of the devil. They appealed to the crown and viceregal officials to prohibit its cultivation and use, arguing that evangelization was difficult enough without the presence of this satanical instrument to further impede their efforts.[105]

Nevertheless, both affirmations as to idolatry and illusion would soon be placed in doubt by the Spanish themselves. Around 1570 the Jesuit José de Acosta (1539? – 1600) considered its effects not illusory but undeniable:

---

[104] *que la coca es cosa sin provecho y muy aparejada para el abuso y superstición de indios ... quiten a los indios el travajo de beneficiar la coca o a lo menos no les fuerzen contra su boluntad* (Ugarte, Rubén Vargas, ed. *Concilios Limenses (1551 – 1772)*, vol. I. Lima: Imprimatur Juan, Cardenal Guevara, 1951 AO, Segundo Consilio, p. 239); L. Grinspoon and J. Bakalaar, 1982, p. 13 and G. Varenne, 1973, p. 375; "In the years 1560-1569 the Government prohibited compulsory labour and the administration of coca because 'the plant is only idolatry and the work of the devil, and appears to give strength only by a deception of the Evil One; it possesses no virtue, but shortens the life of many Indians who at most escape from the forests with ruined health. They should therefore not be compelled to labour and their health and lives should be preserved'" (Lewin, 1964, p. 76).

[105] Gagliano, Joseph A. "The Coca Debate in Colonial Peru," *The Americas*, vol. 20, no. 1 (Jul 1963), Cambridge University Press, jstor.org, p. 44; *Y a los que fueren hallados haber adorado, o hecho sacrificio ... coca o agua, o cuyes, o mollo ... y con ella sean remitidos a do están sus jueces* (Ugarte, 1951 AO, Primer Consilio, Constitución 26a, *En la cual delara la pena ... de los que sacrificaren o idolatraren*, p. 22).

Many serious men consider it mere superstition and a thing of pure imagination. I, to tell the truth, am not persuaded ... because I have seen the effects, that cannot be attributed to imagination, how it is with a fistful of coca they can walk for days without eating anything else, and other similar things.[106]

Somewhat later the Inca Garcilaso de la Vega (Gómez Suárez de Figueroa, 1539 – 1616), born in the Viceroyalty of Peru and whose mother was the daughter of Tupac Hualpa and father the conquistador Sebastián Garcilaso de la Vega y Vargas, allowed himself in his *Comentarios reales* a sarcastic yet practical disquisition on the subject:

But some people ... have said and written many things against the little plant, with no other reason than that the gentiles, in ancient times, and now some wizards and diviners, offered *cuca* to the idols, on which ground these people say that its use ought to be entirely prohibited. Certainly, this would be good counsel if the Indians offered up this and nothing else to the devil. But seeing that the ancient idolaters and modern wizards also sacrifice maize, vegetables, and fruits, whether growing above or under ground, as well as their beverage, cold water, wool, clothes, sheep, and many other things, and as they cannot all be prohibited, neither should the *cuca*.[107]

The Inca Garcilaso possessed some of the largest coca plantations of the Viceroyalty and inherited from his maternal

---

[106] *Muchos hombres graues lo tienen por superſticion ... con vn puño de coca caminar doblan jornadas ſin comer a las veẓes otra coſa, y otras ſemejantes obras* (De Acosta, Padre Ioſeph. <u>Historia Natvral y Moral de las Indias</u>. Madrid: en caſa de Alonſo Martin, 1608 AO, libro quarto, cap. 22, *Del Cacao, y de la Coca*, pp. 252-253).

[107] De la Vega, Garcilasso. <u>First Part of the Royal Commentaries of the Yncas</u>, vol. II, tr. Clements R. Markham. London: Printed for the Hakluyt Society, 1871, Eighth Book, ch. XV, Of the Precious Leaf called Cuca, and of Tobacco, p. 372; *ignorando todas estas cosas han dicho y escrito mucho contra este arbollilo ... y como todas no se les deben quitar tampoco aquella* (D la Vega, Garcilaso. <u>Los Comentarios Reales D Los Incas</u>, vol. II, ed. Horacio H. Urteaga. Lima: Imp. y Libreria Sanmarti y Ca., 1919 AO, Libro Octavo, cap. XV, *De la preciada hoja llamada cuca, y de el tabaco*, p. 352).

ancestors the most lively sympathy toward this plant. His prudence stands out considering that he puts his most intelligent commentary in the mouth of the Jesuit priest, Father Blas Valera (1545 – 1597). Medicinally, De la Vega echoes the sentiments of Dr. Alonso de Huerta and Fray Toribio de Benavente o Motolinia:

There are many other herbs in Peru of such virtue as medicines that, as Father Blas Valera says, if they were all known it would be unnecessary to bring any from Spain, or from anywhere else. But the Spanish doctors think so little of them, that even those that were formerly known to the Indians, are, for the most part, forgotten.[108]

But also he tells of the exploitation of the mines of Potosi, and the formidable fiesta periodically celebrated there (the largest in the world then by volume of transactions) requiring the importation for the use of the miners and their neighbors alone some 100,000 baskets of coca, the equivalent of 1,300 tons of leaves, more than three and a half tons a day. The Spanish administration organized under the name of *la mita* a means of using the Andean labor, initially for the large estates but afterwards established as a general and obligatory system of providing labor for the mines, especially for Potosi.[109] This demanded that all the Indians between 18 and 50 years old must lend a total of 18 months of labor (one for each year and a half) and a good part of the *mita* was employed in caring for the coca plantations.

---

[108] De la Vega, 1871, p. 375; *Otras muchas yerbas hay en el Peru ... de la mayor parte dellas* (De la Vega, 1919, p. 353).

[109] Poma de Ayala, Felipe Guaman. *Nueva Corónica y Buen Gobierno*, vol. I. Caracas: Biblioteca Ayacucho, 1980 AO, Prologo, F. P., p. LXI: *La administración española organizó bajo este nombre [la mita] una forma de utilizar la mano de obra andina, inicialmente para encomiendas ... pero después ... fue establecida como un sistema generalizado y obligatorio de proveer mano de obra para las minas, especialmente para Potosí ...*

THE GENERAL HISTORY OF DRUGS VOLUME 2 PART 2

As with those who labored in the mines of Potosi, some Spaniards were *afficionados* of the leaf personally, and above all, appreciated its qualities to do more work and with less food in the hands of indigenous workers. It was inevitable that the bishops would soon find a *modus vivendi*, and so it happened. The cultivation was tolerated while its use in any kind of religious ceremony remained always condemned, and a tax was levied on any transaction.[110]

On 18 October 1569 a *Real Decreto* of Philip II condemned its use as idolatry and attributed any supposed effects to infernal illusion:

We are informed that the custom which the Peruvian Indians have in using coca and its cultivation cause them grave troubles, for it is used much in idolatrous practices, ceremonies, and witchcraft; and they imagine that by carrying it in their mouth they receive strength and vigor for their work which, according to those who have experimented with it, is an illusion of the devil.[111]

Yet, on 3 October 1572 the *Ordenanzas* issued by Viceroy Francisco Álvarez de Toledo (1515 – 1582) were clearly aimed not at prohibition but at harm reduction:

[He] issued more than fifty additional ordinances as part of his coca reform. ... Toledo ordered that under no circumstances was forced labor to be used in coca cultivation. ... Nor were the planters nor their overseers to compel Indians to work in Andes Province. ... Permanent camayos [workers] who resided in Andes Province

---

[110] Lewin, 1964, p. 76: "All these [earlier] restrictions proved of no avail, and coca became a State monopoly, to pass at the end of the eighteenth century into the hands of private enterprise."

[111] Gagliano, 1963, p. 50; *Somos informado, que de la costumbre que los Indios del Perú tienen en el uso de la Coca ... es ilusion de el Demonio* (Carlos II. *Recopilacion de Leyes de los Reynos de las Indias*, vol. II. Madrid: Por la viuda de D. Joaquin Ibarra, 1791 AO, Libro VI, Titulo XIIII, *Del servicio en coca, y añir, Ley J. Que los Indios, que trabajan en la coca sean bien tratados, y no usen de ella en supersticiones, y hechicerías*, p. 305).

were to receive a minimum annual salary of thirty pesos. The pay of mita workers was to be determined by the justicia of Andes Province. To prevent chicanery, wages were to be paid directly to the Indians instead of their caciques [chiefs]. ... [T]he length of service for mita camayos was kept at twenty-four days. ... Planters were forbidden to induce them to stay longer with promises of large salaries.[112]

The *Ordenanzas* considered the consumption of and traffic in these leaves was necessary for the wellbeing of the Indians. "Toledo ... and other viceregal officials, regarded coca chewing as a vice, albeit a necessary one for the Indians."[113]

An appelate court judge Juan de Matienzo (1520 – 1579) pointed out the obvious existential threat if they banned coca:

If coca were abolished, it is said that the tyranny of the Incas would return. And if it were abolished, the Indians would not go to Potosí. Neither would they work nor mine, and that plate which they would extract, they would bury in their huacas [sacred ceremonial sites] ... And finally, it should be said that if coca is wanting, there will be no Peru ..., the land will become depopulated, and the Indians will return to their pagan ways.[114]

With such counsel, Philip II also formally recognized in an *Ordenanza* of 11 June 1573 that the cultivation of coca was a great benefit primarily because with coca they could extract so much silver

---

[112] Gagliano, 1963, p. 53; Levillier, Roberto, ed. *Gobernantes del Peru*, Cartas y Papeles, Siglo XVI, vol. VIII. Madrid: Imprenta de Juan Pueyo, 1925, *Ordenanzas del Virrey Toledo relativas al cultivo de la Coca*, pp. 15-35.

[113] Gagliano, 1963, p. 57.

[114] Gagliano, 1963, p. 52; *y si se le quitasen no yrian a Potosi, ni trabajarian, ni sacarian plata y los que sacasen enterrarian en sus guaeas ... finalmente querer que no aya coca, es querer que no aya Peru y se despueble la tierra y los Indios se buelvan a su infidelidad* (Matienzo, Juan. *Gobierno del Perú*. Buenos Aires: Compañía Sud-Americana de Billetes de Banco, 1910 AO, cap. 44, p. 90)

from the mines *(por la mucha plata, que por su causa se saca de las minas)*.[115] Instead of prohibiting the drug, the new law prohibited "the plantations from packing more than 500 baskets *(cestos)* of coca in any one harvest season."[116] More importantly, some ten percent of the value of the sales of this substance belonged to the clergy and this tithe quickly became the single most important source of income for the bishops and canons of Lima and Cuzco. "[T]he greater part of the revenue of the bishops and canons of the cathedral of Cuzco is derived from the tithe of the *cuca* leaves; and they enrich many Spaniards who trade with them."[117]

With this there arose a situation not exempt of ambiguities. The popular use of the plant increased, relaxing the severe controls of the Incas. But this did not mean that it entered into the orbit of the decorous. It was a custom of the miserable natives, which only little by little shows up in the most favored social circles. The Sevillian doctor Nicolás Monardes (1493 – 1588) gave before the end of the sixteenth century the first botanical description of the plant and lauded its use by the Indians to "taketh the hunger and thirft from them: they fay that

---

[115] Carlos II, 1791, Libro VI, Titulo XIIII, Ley ij. *Ordenanza de la Coca*, p. 306: *El trato de la Coca, que se cria, y beneficia en las Provincias de el Perú, es uno de los mayores, y que mas las enriquecen ... Que ninguna persona pueda tener chacra de mas de quinientos cestos de cosecha de Coca en cada mita ....*

[116] Gagliano, 1963, p. 58; *Que ninguna persona pueda tener chacra de mas de quinientos cestos de cosecha de Coca en cada mita* (Carlos II, 1791, Libro VI, Titulo XIIII, Ley ij. *Ordenanza de la Coca*, p. 306).

[117] De la Vega, 1871, p. 372; *la mayor parte de la renta del obispo, y de los canónigos, y de los demás ministros de la iglesia catedral del Cosco, es de los diesmos de las hojas de la cuca; y muchos españoles han enriquecideo y enriquecen con el trato y contrato desta yerba* (De la Vega, 1919, p. 352).

they receiue fubftaunce thereby, as though they dyd eate meate."[118]
But he also notices that when "they will make themfelues drunke, and
be out of iudgement, they mingle with the *Coca* the leaues of the
Tabaco, and chewe them altogether, and goe as they were out of their
wittes, or as if they were drunke."[119]

The priest Felipe Guaman Poma de Ayala (1536? – 1616)
illustrated neatly the dichotomy. On the one hand, chewing coca
leaves was idolatry and vice: "All those who chew coca are sorcerers
who speak to demons; whether drunk or not, they go crazy by chewing
coca. May God save us. Sacraments cannot be given to those who
chew coca."[120] On the other hand he compares the Indian *coquero* to
the Spanish *tabaquero*:

The Inca created coca and taught the Indians how to chew it. This is an idolatrous
habit. They say it sustains users, but I do not believe this. It is a rather wicked vice,
like the Spaniards who smoke tobacco, an impertinent vice. But a drunken Indian
who chews coca is certainly a public sorcerer and priest of the Inca.[121]

---

[118] Monardes, Nicolas. Joyfvll Newes Out of the New-found World, Englifh'd by
John Frampton. London: Printed by E. Allde, by the afsigne of Bonhans Norton,
1596 AO, The Thyrde Part of the Thinges that are Brought from the Weft Indais, f.
102r; *les quita la hambre y la fed ... como fi comieffen* (Monardes, Nicolas. *Primera y Segvnda
y Tercera Partes de La Historia Medicinal*. Sevilla: En cafa de Alonfo Efcriuano, 1574
AO, Segunda Parte. *De las cofas que traen de nřas Indias, que firuen al vfo de medicina, De la
Coca*, pp. 114-115).

[119] Monardes, 1596, f. 102 1/r; Monardes, 1574, p. 115: *Quando fe quieren emborrachar ...
como vn hombre borracho ....*

[120] Poma de Ayala, Felipe Guaman. The First New Chronicle and Good
Government, tr., ed. Roland Hamilton. Austin: University of Texas Press, 2009
(1615) AO, [278 (280)], p. 214; *Todos los que comen coca son hechiceros que hablan con los
demonios ... dar sacramento al que come coca* (Poma de Ayala, 1980, 278 [280], p. 197).

[121] Poma de Ayala, 2009 (1615) AO, [332 (334)], p. 264; *Como el Inga inventó y le enseñó a
comer coca ... hechicero público y pontífice del Inga* (Poma de Ayala, 1980, 332 [334], p. 238).

Ultimately, if it was not used for work, the mastication of coca leaves was an unauthorized social activity.[122]

3. The Instructive Case of *Maté*.

It seems that the leaves (untoasted) of *Ilex paraguariensis* were employed as a medicinal plaster by the Tupi-Guarani culture and (toasted) as a stimulant for daily use by various other ethnic groups. However, one of the first chroniclers of Paraguay, the Jesuit ethnographer and historian Pedro Lozano (1697 – 1752), agreed with the governor who burned the herb in the public square of Buenos Aires saying that "this herb will be the fatal ruin of your numberless country and that Spaniards should never have discovered the pernicious use of it."[123]

Padre Antonio Ruiz de Montoya (1585 – 1652), who lived with the natives for three decades, also agreed with this thesis:

I carefully inquired about its origin from Indians who were eighty to a hundred years old. I learned as a certain fact that in their youth the herb was not drunk or even known except by a great sorcerer or magician who trafficked with the devil. The devil showed him the herb and told him to drink it whenever he wanted to consult him.[124]

---

[122] Van Dyke and Byck, 1982, p. 103.

[123] *que esta yerba ha de ser fatal ruina ... el pernicioso uso de ella* (Lozano, Pedro. *Historia de la Conquista del Paraguay*, vol. I, ed. Andres Lamas. Buenos Aires: Casa Editora Imprenta Popular, 1873 AO, ch. VIII, *Dase noticia en gernal de la fertilidad de estas provincias y se trata largamente de la yerba que llaman del Paraguay*, pp. 201-202); Perez de Barradas, 1957, p. 180.

[124] Ruiz de Montoya, Antonio. The Spiritual Conquest, tr. C. J. McNaspy et al. St. Louis, MO: The Institute of Jesuit Sources, 1993 (1639), pp. 42-43; *Digo, q con todo cuidado he bufcado fu origen entre Indios de 80. y 100. años ... q quando quifieffe confuicarle beuiefffe aquella yerua* (Padre Antonio Ruiz. *Conquista Espiritval*. Madrid: En la imprenta del Reyno, 1639 AO, ch. 7, *Ida a aquella mifsion del Padre Antonio Ruiz, y trata de la yerua que llaman del Paraguay*, f. 9); *Antonio Ruiz de Montoya, que tuvo tanta esperiencia*

As a consequence of this alarming news, and not before consulting with the *best* doctors of Milan, cardinal and archbishop Federico Borromeo (1564 – 1631) wrote one letter to the bishop of Paraguay and another to the founder of the first Jesuit missions in the province, exhorting them to put every effort into "uprooting such a pernicious evil as the use of this herb with great damage for the health of the souls and bodies."[125]

However, the Company of Jesus had anticipated the present-day prosperous exploitation of the product (around a half million tons annually) and nurtured the idea of propagating *maté* in Europe, competing with the Mexican cacao, and with tea and coffee imported from the East; otherwise, this was reasonable even on pharmacological terms, since the principal stimulative alkaloid of *maté* is almost identical with those in tea, coffee, guarana, cola nut and chocolate.

There began then to be divulged very different news about the herb, preceded by legends of apostolic voyages to the Americas. At the beginning of the seventeenth century Gaspar de Escalona Agüero (1598 – 1659) of the *Real Audiencia* of Chile, added a surprising piece of data to these pedantries in his *Gazophilacium Regium Perubicum*: "[I]t is the general opinion in the region [the provinces of Paraguay] that Saint Bartholomew discovered and showed [*hierba maté*] to the natives."[126]

---

de las cosas de los indios del Paraguay, entre quienes vivió treinta años, y escribe que habiendo inquirido, con todo diligencia ... cuando quisiese escuchar sus oráculos (Lozano, 1873, p. 204).

[125] á que ponga todo empeño en desarraigar mal tan pernicioso, como el usar dicha yerba con grande daño de la salud de las almas y de los cuerpos (Lozano, 1873, p. 214).

[126] es general la opinion en aquella Region, que San Bartholomé la mostró, y descubrió á sus naturales (Escalona, Gaspare de. *Gazophilacium Regium Perubicum*. Matriti: Ex Typographia Blasii Roman, 1775 AO, libro II, part. II, cap. XXIX, Yerva del Paraguay, p. 239); es general opinion en las provincias del Paraguay que san Bartolome la mostro y descubrio a los naturales (Lozano, 1873, pp. 202-203; Lozano calls this very doubtful (*muy dudoso*) and can find no mention of it); Perez de Barradas, 1957, p. 181.

This general opinion, and the edifying content linked to it, caused the bishop of Asunción to vacillate in his policy of intransigence.

Some decades later the traditions were considerably clearer; not only did there exist an agreement that one of the companions of Christ (not Bartholomew but Thomas) had visited these lands to instruct the natives in the use of the leaves of this plant but that he also purified its ancient Satanic element by toasting it (like the bonfire purified apostasy). In 1667, summarizing the reigning opinion, a small book by the attorney Diego de Zeballos called _Tratado del Recto uso de la Yerba del Paraguay_ was published. There we can read:

the apostle Saint Thomas discovered the use of _maté_ and even gave it its power; arriving from Brasil, preaching the gospel in the province of Mbacarayú, he found forests filled with these trees, whose leaves were a deadly poison; but toasted by the holy apostle, they lost in his hands and in the fire, all their noxiousness, leaving them an effective antidote. And for this reason they say the Indians always toasted the herb to use it, because the saint taught them how.[127]

When this book circulates in Asunción there is a _corvea_ related with _maté_ for the indigenous. The botanical work of the Jesuits had flourished in cultivating _hierba maté_ plantations, with better quality every year. The unbelieving apostle _par excelence_ (Thomas, the disciple who demanded to put his finger in the wound) is now the impeccable validator of the plant, which alleviates the poverty of so many. A _Real Cedula_ of 1679 shows that the Jesuit missions in Santa Fe and Buenos Aires sold 12,000 _arrobas_ of the herb, subtracting from this only the tribute to the Crown, to adorn their churches and the services for the people.[128]

---

[127] _descubrio su uso y aun le dio la virtud santo Tomas apostol .... Y por esta razon decian los indios que siempre tuestan la yerba para usarla_ (Lozano, 1873, p. 203).

[128] _porque con la plata que produce vendida en Santa Fé ó Buenos Aires pagan el tributo que como_

The diabolic herb is now the healthful tea of Paraguay. Having passed from a vehicle of apostasy by means of an effective antidote (*eficaz antídoto*, in the words of Zeballos) to a therapeutic panacea, it then ends by becoming a profane stimulant, like coffee and cocoa. This instructive history is not complete without taking into account what happened while *maté* was severely prohibited. According to Padre Lozano: "It grew in such a way that in a few years the use or abuse of the plant only in the city of Asunción, there was consumed fourteen to fifteen thousand *arrobas* annually by 1620; being then a city that hardly counted five hundred Spanish inhabitants."[129]

---

vasallos deben á su magestad ... por real cédula del año de 1679, bajen cada año doce mil arrobas (Lozano, 1873, p. 207).

[129] *Cundió de tal manera en pocos años ... se contaban quinientos vecinos españoles* (Lozano, 1873, p. 205); Perez de Barradas, 1957, p. 182; One arroba is equal to roughly twenty-four to thirty-six pounds depending on the region (Jarman, B. G. and R. Russell, chief eds. The Oxford Spanish Dictionary, fourth ed. Oxford, UK: Oxford University Press, 2008, p. 67).

Figure 118. *Maté y bombilla* in Argentinian silver.

Figure 119. *L'Apothicaire* (The Apothecary), oil painting by
Gabriël Metsu (1624 – 1667), *Musée du Louvre.*

13
The Transition Toward Modernity

The Greek and Roman gods held sway in the realm of nature ....
Fortunate campaigns ... created in Athens and Rome an
aristocracy of wealth and military glory .... The masses
then readily and willingly ceded power ... to the
aristocrats .... Soon the [power] freely granted
to the rulers was upheld by force ....
-- Hegel, Theologische Jugendschriften[1]

---

[1] Hegel, Friedrich. On Christianity: Early Theological Writings, Knox, T. M. and Richard Kroner, trs. NY: Harper & Brothers, 1948 AO, How Christianity Conquered Paganism, pp. 155-156; Nohl, Herman, ed. *Hegel's Theologifche Jugendfchriften*. Tubingen: Berlag von J. C. B. Mohr (Paul Siebeck), 1907 AO, *Unterfchied zwifchen griechifcher Bhantafie und chriftlicher pofitiver Religion*, pp. 222-223: *Ihre Götter herrichten im Reiche der Natur ... Uebermacht mit Gewalt behauptet ....*

The motives, both tacit and expressed, which had kept the use of non-alcoholic drugs in Europe hidden underground, are superseded by stronger ones beginning around the middle of the seventeenth century. To the reasons already alluded to earlier one can add now a more active commerce with the Far East. Opium will become an important article in this overseas exchange.

Infernal substances, heroic remedies, goods for a maritime trade, the plants and drugs of paganism emerge into the light of day. Although they are still rigorously prohibited as vehicles for *travel*, an estate consisting of doctors, pharmacists and pharmaceutical chemists employs and distributes them in ever more active preparations. At the same moment, new drugs with an extraordinary future appear, which are received with a marked ambivalence at least in the beginning.

Drugs always were an important means of communication between distant cultures. But from this moment forward entire continents import and export them massively, and with this one detects the first seeds of xenophobia linked to one or another substance. The Chinese measures against certain European alcohols (which will be promptly followed by similar prohibitions on tobacco), the clash between Christians and Ottomans in the Mediterranean, and the reception given to the drugs of the New World and to Arabian coffee (to mention only the most obvious) unleash a mobilization of energy and investment in keeping with the horizons opened by the increasingly European control of the seas and their colonial policies ashore. But before describing all this, it's necessary to close the books on the era just concluded, profiling its relationship with the previous and the one to come.

CH. 13 THE TRANSITION TOWARD MODERNITY

A.   Demonomania and Toxicomania

The treatise _De la demonomania des sorciers_, published by the French demonologist Jean Bodin in 1580 [see Ch. 12, p. 737, e.g.], established a direct relationship between drugs and witchcraft, something that occurred in the works of various other jurisconsults as well.[2] We also saw that the simple possession of _ointments_ occasioned an automatic and unassailable presumption of witchcraft, even though the possessors and users were not linked to that profession nor attended witchcraft ceremonies. The pathetic case of the wife of the notary mentioned by Bartholomew della Spina [see GHDV2P1 Ch. 10, p. 647 et seq] is a typical example of the dilemma, certainly terrible, in which spouses, family members, domestics and masters found themselves when, upon opening a door, they encountered someone undergoing a _voyage_.

Even so, the duality demonomania/toxicomania seems to have been ignored as the persecution was only directed _circumstantially_ against drugs. To the inquisitor it mattered very little the natural origins of witchcraft, and he even preferred to think that the unguents and potions were pharmacologically laughable, because his business was not to verify what the witch knew or did, but to mythologically tame the other members of society, convincing them that they were safe thanks to him. In effect, the legislation against witchcraft was never really directed against the witches and never was meant to dissuade them either. It can be better understood as a means to comfort the

---

[2] N. Remy (_Daemonolatreiae_, 1596) and H. Boquet (_Discovrs Execrable des Sorciers_, 1603) [see ch. 12, pp. 799-800]. The fifth book (_De Maleficis et eorvm Deceptionibvs_) of the German theologian Johannes Nider's _Formicarius_ (1437) formed the basis of Heinrich Kramer's _Malleus_ (Nyder, Ioannis. _Myrmecia Bonorvm siue Formicarivs_. Dvaci: Baltazaris Billeri, 1602 AO, liber quintus, p. 331 et seq), for example.

others generally, making them feel fraternally united before a deviant. Thanks to this characteristic, which it shares with all legislation against spiritual plagues, the crusade was indifferent to the fact that the number of those infected should increase rather than decrease with the persecution. The more it should seem like a civil war *sine die* and without quarter, the more comforted (and more dissuaded from any inconstancy before the enemy) would feel the respectable.

This had the advantage of *disassociating* the real facts of witchcraft (the empirical knowledge of the herbalists, the survival of pagan rituals, shamanism, orgiastic and ecstatic communion) from a persecutorial mythology explicable only as a response to social and political changes. That the devil worshippers should be plant worshippers was an accident and even an unforeseen consequence making the inquisitioners uncomfortable, because it was more convenient to persecute someone raised up by supernatural powers than someone supported by natural powers, simply botanical. In essence, the crusade was a force to strengthen control at moments when the loss of prestige and power of the clergy and nobility encouraged the growth of an apocalyptic threat, completely independent of a greater or lesser consumption of psychoactive substances.

All that being said, this disassociation ignores two essential factors. One is that from the thirteenth to the eighteenth centuries witchcraft did not just represent the old pagan ceremonies and forgotten demons, but also an original and progressively vigorous resistance to the Christian conception of life. The other factor, even more important, is derived from previous Christian history. If we say, for example, that the basis of the persecution was the power of the devil and not the power of the drugs, we are saying something specific, but which at the same time ignores Christianity's own diabolical genealogy as historical fact. Satan is a common name for Dionysius and other deities of natural religions, of an ecstatic and orgiastic type, which Christianity demolished in the first centuries of its existence, not only persecuting their adherents and prohibiting their rites, but also erasing their memory at the most effective level, which was to burn entire libraries and destroy specific books.

From the prohibition of opium as the filth of the devil down to the many-layered changes of fortune in the seventeenth century which accompanied the conversion of *maté* into an apostolic gift snatched from infernal claws, *apostasy* and the consumption of reputedly entheogenic substances are perfectly parallel acts, confused over and over again. Not all apostasy supposes the ritual use of drugs, but all ritual use of drugs is apostasy, of course. Perhaps the devil has more power than drugs, but the power of drugs clearly arises from the devil.

For the same reason, it is important to distinguish a sector of society with the knowledge and practice of pharmacology from a delirious mythology imposed by a persecution, based above all on other benefits. Nevertheless, it cannot be denied that from the fifth century onwards (at least from the Augustinian thesis of the *diabolical illusion* to explain the phenomenon of metamorphosis), the witchcraft of possession and shamanism, the pagan initiation rites, orgies and the whole universe linked to drugs constitute a recurring *justification* for the campaigns undertaken for their extermination. It is not often stated precisely which ones nor why, but there exist *maleficent* herbs; neither does it appear to be known which ones nor why, although there exist *infernal* unguents; in equal measure it is a thing obscure as to which ones and why, although there exist *satanic* plants. The fact of not tackling directly the question, with precise analytic categories, does not mean there were doubts with regards to the foundation of the prohibition, but only that the theme itself is obscene, like sexuality, and that to confront it offends. This is intrinsically Christian.

Figure 120. *Der. Cor Capen. Ein Gvt. Iar* (To the chorists a good year),
black quill pen drawing, Hans Baldung Grien (1484/5 -1545),
Albertina Museum, Vienna, Austria.

CH. 13 THE TRANSITION TOWARD MODERNITY

1.   The Origins of the Divergence.   Before and after
the Renaissance (in reality down to today) drugs, concupiscence and
satanism are three sides of a triangle inscribed upon the heart of
apostolic faith as a single unpardonable sin.[3]   In my judgment, the
singular intensity presented by the concatenation of these elements,
distinct and well separated in other conceptions of the world, explains
(at least in part) what was previously defined as the entheogenic
promise betrayed [see GHDV2P1 Ch. 8, p. 485 for a more in-depth
discussion]. In contrast with the legalism of the Mosaic religion, Christ
preached love as the divine essence and proposed an unconditional
reconciliation between men. One aspect of this reconciliation appears
in the proposal to celebrate his memory with a banquet of bread and
wine, which schematically unites the Eleusinian and Dionysiac
traditions.

On the other hand, the subject is also more profound. Though
it's very difficult to separate the original message of Jesus from its later
perversions, what for him is characteristically ethical is not the

---

[3] Against this, Jesus argues that the unpardonable sin is to attribute miracles, whether
of nature or his own, to Satan. See for example, Matthew 12: 31: "Wherefore I say
unto you, All manner of sin and blasphemy shall be forgiven unto men: but the
blasphemy *against* the *Holy Ghost* shall not be forgiven unto men" or Matthew 12: 32:
"And whosoever speaketh a word against the Son of man, it shall be forgiven him:
but whosoever speaketh against the Holy Ghost, it shall not be forgiven him, neither
in this world, neither in the *world* to come" (KJV, blueletterbible.org, hereinafter,
BLB). [The chapter begins with the disciples walking "through the corn" (Matthew
12: 1) and eating what they plucked on the Sabbath. The chapter then records
complaints that Jesus was healing on the Sabbath and finally that his healing was due
to Satan. Corn, of course, refers to wheat, rye, barley and cereal grasses in general
and ergot (*Claviceps purpurea*) parasitizes many of these, but there is no evidence that
the disciples were deliberately harvesting ergot.]

sentence that says *one should love one's neighbor as oneself*, which already appears textually in the Pentateuch:

You shall not hate your brother in your heart. You shall surely rebuke your fellow, but you shall not bear a sin on his account. You shall neither take revenge from nor bear a grudge against the members of your people; you shall love your neighbour as yourself. I am the Lord.[4]

The first difference which separates Jesus from Moses is the lifting of the restriction on the message to only a special people, amplifying one's *neighbor* to any human being; however, the second and decisive distinction is knowing that the act itself of judging also condemns the protagonist.[5] Jesus continually places man apart from the law, opposing sentiment to commandment, to intolerance *a moral disposition that does not require struggle.*[6] Finally, lack of virtue for him is to

---

[4] *Vayikra* – Leviticus 19: 17-18, chabad.org.

[5] Matthew 7: 1-2: "Judge not, that ye be not judged. For with what judgment ye judge, ye shall be judged: and with what measure ye mete, it shall be measured to you again" (BLB); Luke 6: 38: "Give, and it whall be given unto you; good measure, pressed down, and shaken together, and running over, shall men give into your bosom. For with the same measure that ye mete withal it shall be measured to you again" (BLB); John 5: 22: "For the Father judgeth no man, but hath committed all judgment unto the Son" (BLB). That the Son should judge signifies that the time has arrived of brotherhood, the royal fraternity.

[6] *nicht die Unterftützung der moralifchen Gefinnung durch Reigung, fondern eine geneigte moralifche Gefinnung d. h. eine moralifche Gefinnung ohne Kampf* (Nohl, 1907, *Der Geift des Chriftentums und fein Echicgfal*, p. 268, ft. a); Hegel, 1948, The Spirit of Christianity and its Fate, ii. The Moral Teachings of Jesus, p. 214. Knox does not translate note [a] on page 268 of Nohl: "Nohl printed in footnotes a number of passages which Hegel had written and then deleted; these .. have been omitted from the translation ... (p. v)," perhaps because they closely restate the text. A rough translation of the note is "not the support of the moral conviction by inclination, but an inclined moral conviction, i.e., a moral agreement without a struggle." The footnoted sentence reads: "This

see in someone else some act externally obedient to some rule, arrogating to oneself the right to denounce their spontaneity.

As such this proposal was really very distant from anything that could have been called ethical up to then. Afterwards it fell into the hands of an extremely paranoid Puritanism, the mystery at its core or the original mystery converted into an implacable mechanism of control. The reconciliation of the Father and the Son, of yesterday and tomorrow, ceded its place to a life split in two by the battle between the carnal and the spiritual. *Thou shalt not judge* was transformed into the most rigid orthodoxy known for centuries. The Jews believed the law was supreme, while the ethical was meticulous obedience to it. Jesus opposed to this dry rigor the beautiful soul and its spontaneity, violating the rule of resting on the Sabbath, dispensing forgiveness, postponing the offer before the altar pending a reconciliation with one's brother.[7] The Paulist orientation which ended up being imposed

---

supplement [fulfillment] he [Jesus] goes on to exhibit in several laws. This expanded content we may call an inclination so to act as the laws may command, i.e., a unification of inclination with the law whereby the latter loses its form as law (p. 214)." An external law has been internalized.

[7] Matthew 5: 23-24: "Therefore if thou bring thy gift to the altar, and there rememberest that thy brother hath ought against thee; Leave there thy gift before the altar, and go thy way; first be reconciled to thy brother, and then come and offer thy gift" (BLB). Compare Matthew 6: 28-34: "And why take ye thought for raiment? Consider the lilies of the field, how they grow; they toil not, neither do they spin: Any yet I say unto you, That even Solomon in all his glory was not arrayed like one of these. Wherefore, if God so clothe the grass of the field, which to day is, and to morrow is cast into the oven, *shall he* not much more *clothe* you, O ye of little faith? Therefore take no thought, saying, what shall we eat? or, What shall we drink? or, Wherewithal shall we be clothed? (For after all these things do the Gentiles seek:) for your heavenly Father knoweth that ye have need of all these things. But seek ye first the kingdom of God, and his righteousness; and all these things shall be added unto you. Take therefore no thought for the morrow: for the morrow shall take thought

wanted to convert law into a higher power, corrupting ethics as much as law.

On the level most directly related to the alteration of consciousness, Christianity was established as a *spiritual* religion opposed to a *natural* one, a thing that in practice means faith, sobriety and ritual *versus* mystical experiences, intensity and autonomy. As with the history of its conflict with the ancient natural religions of Europe and the Mediterranean (a catechism renewed in each new continent), Christianity sweeps away a convention at once indelible and obscure about demonic ends disseminated by a terrestrial plant for the pleasure of the witches, the old black adversaries to its white magic. Thanks to this mystical/persecutorial complex, from the thirteenth to the eighteenth centuries the difference between the *pharmakon* and the *phamakos* is erased, since whoever employs an unguent is self-included in the catalog of possible sacrificial lambs, whose fulmination decontaminates the social body.

2.   The Terms of the Crisis.   It is not exact to insist on the opposition of Christianity to the recreational and ethical use of drugs, based upon the advantages of affliction, the condemnation of hedonism and the fact of men and women not being the owners of their own minds and bodies. From an orthodox perspective, it is not this drug or that drug, but all psychoactive substances (distinct from the alcoholic beverages) that are inadmissible as vehicles of recreation, ecstasy or euthanasia, *indulging* a medical use when both doctor and patient should appear to be socially and doctrinally untouchable. We shall soon see how neatly this mechanism works in Europe and the Muslim world with regards to tobacco and coffee, precisely due to the actions of high Catholic ecclesiastics and Islamic preachers.

---

for the things of itself. Sufficient unto the day is the evil thereof' (BLB).

As a consequence, any response to the question as to whether or not there is some kernel of similarity between the crusade against the demonomania of the witches and the crusade against toxicomania should carry with it a warning. In the crusade which we have been examining, the use of drugs is not set forth as something related to its chemistry nor dependent upon notions of psychopharmacology. In this specific sense, the persecution of the witches (like non-witchcraft prohibitions that weighed upon opium and the solanaceas in different times and places) can only be considered a very vague precedent for a crusade explicitly focused upon *the drug*. In fact, until the witch hunt began to subside there was no chemistry, while psychopharmacology stands out by its absence. The most serious attempts in this sense (which we owe to Porta) ended before the Holy See, and the caution with which Laguna expresses himself, for example, demonstrates to what point scientific discourse on similar themes was dangerous. The *crux* of the question resides then in deciding if the contemporary crusade is or is not something really born out of the chemistry, pharmacology and science in the widest sense. But this cannot be decided before examining its genesis and development, so it's opportune to leave the answer in suspense until having examined more closely a similar initiative.

For now at the end of the seventeenth century, what shows up is a crisis of values. If from a political point of view, liberty of conscience begins to be reclaimed in place of orthodoxy, the distinction between morality and law instead of a self-interested amalgam, examination by reason instead of admissibility by faith, then from the particular perspective of drugs it simply appears risible to believe in the existence of impious plants, drinks concocted by Satan and other commonplaces during the previous millennium and a half. The duality drugs/concupiscence is not defended, prohibition is not commingled with recreational use, nor is pain admitted to come from

God. On the contrary, opium will come be considered to be the greatest divine gift in the pharmacopoeia thanks to its analgesic and sedative qualities. One observes everywhere a return to pagan criteria, not only because drugs once again come to be considered as things neutral in themselves (completely indifferent for the law and left to the understanding of their users) but also because with regards to them a lively scientific curiosity becomes a very frequent theme, in contrast to the previous silence.

Before the advent of monotheisms with aspirations to world domination, never did the legislator or priest dare to tread upon the terrain of substances capable of altering the soul. Everything related to this (like that related with the daily routine, diet and intimacy in general, beginning with sex) was always considered a matter left to the discretion of the individual, without prejudice to what the customs might suggest in each place concerning one habit or another. It seems worthy of mention that while the authority of ecclesiastical hierarchy over civil society was unquestioned not a single new drug was discovered, while from now on discoveries are going to be found at a vertiginous pace. Without doubt this depends on scientific progress, but scientific progress cannot be achieved unless first discursive reason should be freed from its limited role as handmaiden to faith.

Though both Islam and Christianity coincide in assuming the right to dogmatize on the subject, it's clear that they exhibit different attitudes, which can be nuanced as relative permissibility and radical intolerance. At the same moment, just as intolerance is distinguished from permission, civil liberty can be distinguished from tolerance. If one can say that Islam initially was permissive, then now one observes that European society begins to be simply, free.

B.   The New Spice Route

At the beginning of the fifteenth century, fundamentally via the Muslims, Venice controlled the commerce in spices coming from the Hindustan peninsula, Cathay and the Eastern Indies. Its ships search for them in ports around the Black Sea and Alexandria, where they

Figure 121. Woodcut from Hieronymus Brunschwygk [Brunschwig], the _Liber de arte Diftillandi de Compofitis_. Straussberg: Johann Gruninger, 1512 AO, ch. xxxvi, f. xciii (l).

arrive by land following the torturous silk routes. But these routes[8] are exposed to greater and greater difficulties in this and the following century, as if the enormous natural obstacles already existing were of no importance.

The fall of the Yuan dynasty (1279 – 1368), the black death and other plagues, brigandage, the hostility toward the Christians by the Ottomans after their capture of Constantiople (1453), and the collapse of the Mameluke empire (1517) closed many of them. This increased the dependence of the trade on Alexandria, the only relatively secure enclave for finding spices, which were then resold at exorbitant prices in the markets of the north and east of Europe.

The privileged Venetian business continued until a combination of Italian capitalists and Portuguese mariners managed to explore the western coasts of Africa, discovering a southern passage to Asia in 1488 with the Portuguese navigator Bartolomeu Dias (1450 – 1500), a decade later arriving in Calicut by sea in 1498 with the expedition of Vasco da Gama (1460 – 1524). Over the next hundred years only the Portuguese navy takes satisfactory advantage of this access, which when combined with an exploration of the sources of gold in the region of Niger converts Portugal into an economic power of the first magnitude.

However, in 1599 and 1600 a Dutch fleet commanded by Jacob Corneliszoon van Neck (1564 – 1638) managed to bring to Europe from the Spice Islands (the Moluccas and the Malayan

---

[8] In reality, there were four main routes: (a) the northern land route from Xi'an to Kashgar and Turkmenistan with a branch to the Black Sea, (b) the southern land route through the Karakoram mountains, Pakistan, Afghanistan, Turkmenistan arriving in Syria and Turkey, (c) the southwestern land route through Yunnan province, Burma and Bangladesh, then by sea from the Ganges delta, and (d) the southern maritime route from the South China Sea, through the Strait of Malacca, across the Indian Ocean to the Persian Gulf.

archipelago) a cargo so rich in clove, nutmeg, mace, cinnamon and pepper that it earned him a profit [so it has been said] of some 400 percent. The English response was immediate and in 1600 Queen Elizabeth conceded a monopoly concession to the British East India Company. This was followed by a Dutch homologue, the *Vereenigde Oostindische Compagnie* (VOC), two years later.

From that point onward there is a commercial war (and at times a military one) between the Portuguese, English and Dutch, which ends with the first enclosed in the enclaves of Goa and Macao, granting to the other two a Solomonic division of their zones of influence: the British interests take root in India and Ceylon while the Dutch rule in large part the Eastern Indies. Centered in Batavia (Jakarta), the Dutch can be distinguished from their rivals by looking for commercial monopolies instead of kingdoms, far removed from any zeal for a religious or political empire.

The mercantile repercussions of the Portuguese discovery could not have been greater for Europe and the Mameluke (and later the Ottoman) Empire. The Muslim control over the traffic in spices was liquidated and with it sank the Venetian commercial monopoly. At the same time European businessmen and investors obtained a rich variety of goods, a source of insuperable earnings then.

The transcendence of all this for the commerce in opium derives from the fact that European manufacturers lacked an Asian demand, and the only payment then admissible were the precious metals. Because of this the Portuguese founded their African posts, accessible to the trans-Saharan caravans, which managed to bring there thousands of slaves as well as almost a ton of gold annually, an effective means of exchange. However, the system was expensive and shortsighted, until the Europeans hit on the possibility of transporting the opium produced in the south of the Iberian peninsula and that from Asia Minor by sea. The success of the initiative bypassed altogether the difficulties of transport in Persia and Turkey. Portugal was once again the pioneer followed shortly after by the Dutch and the English.

This resulted in a valuable trade good, one capable of multiplying the normal margin of commercial profit up to previously unthinkable extremes when blessed with a foreign [Chinese] prohibition. The ever more rigorous prohibition of opium in late-Qing dynasty China will induce the English to till great plantations of poppies in their colonial Asiatic domains in the nineteenth century, with consequences that will be examined later. For now we arrive at the first steps of this operation.

1.   The Portuguese Doctors and Botanists.   During   his voyage along the Malabar coasts (1511), the Portuguese explorer (who later sails with Magellan) Duarte Barbosa (1480 – 1521) discovered that opium from the Mediterranean basin was a product which would allow a good return in the Far East.[9] From that moment Portugal carried, on its expeditions and established in its colonies, men capable of investigating the plants and the customs of the new territories. The royal apothecary Tomé Pires (c. 1465 – c. 1540) was sent to Canton as an expert in the knowledge of medicinal plants, and ended becoming

---

[9] Barbosa, Duarte. <u>Description of the Coasts of East Africa and Malabar in the beginning of the sixteenth century</u>, tr. Henry E. J. Stanley. London: Printed for the Hakylut Society, 1866 AO, pp. 86, 177, 184, 188: "[A]nd they import ... much anfani which is opium .... Copper, quicksilver, vermilion, opium, and many Cambay goods fetch a good price .... Many Moorish ships ... bring thither ... opium, copper, scarlet cloth .... [O]pium, Cambay stuffs, and all these goods fetch a high price at this place." See also Barbosa, Duarte. <u>*Livro Em que dá relação do que viu e ouviu no Oriente*</u>. Lisboa: *Divisão de Publicações e Biblioteca, Agência Geral das Colónias*, 1946 AO, pp. 42, 199, 219, e. g.: *muito anfião e panes de Cambaia; e tudo isto, tem grande valia neste reino de Anseão* ....

the ambassador of his country to China in 1516. In a letter/report of 27 January 1516 to King Manuel on the drugs he discovered he mentions opium, where it grows, and distinguishes Theban from Bengali: "Opium – Opium we call here *amfião*. It grows in Thebes, a city of the kingdom of Cairo. It grows in Aden, in Cambay, in the kingdom of *Cõus*, which is on the Bengal mainland. This is a great merchandise ... consumed in great quantity, and very valuable."[10]

Some decades later, the physician and naturalist Garcia da Orta (1501/2 – 1568) in his 1563 *Coloquios dos simples e drogas da India* (Colloquies on the Simples & Drugs of India), (in which appear the first verses of his friend the Portuguese national poet Luís Vaz de Camões [Camoens, 1524/5 – 1580])[11] describes opium consumption in Goa and its different kinds:

RUANO

I should like to have accurate information about the Amfiam which is what the people of this land use, and we call Opium. Whence comes such a quantity as is used here, and how much is taken each day?

ORTA

The Amfiam is the opium, and as for its being much used to eat among many people, it is really eaten in small quantity, though much is required in trade to supply all the things it is in demand for. If it is not used there is danger of death ensuing, so that in the land where it is wanting its price is very dear, and there is a very strong desire for

---

[10] Coresão, Armando, tr. The Suma Oriental of Tomé Pires, vol. II. London: Printed for the Hakylut Society, 1944 AO, Appendix I, Letter of Tomé Pires to King Manuel, p. 513; *Carta de Tomé Pires Para o Rei*, 27 Jan. 1516, *Corpo Cronológico, Parte I, mç. 19, no. 102, Arquivo Nacional Torre do Tombo*, DGLab, digitarq.arquivos.pt: *Opío* ....

[11] Orta, Garcia da. *Coloquios dos Simples e Drogas da India*, vol. I. Lisboa: Imprensa Nacional, 1891 AO, pp. 7-9; see also Orta, Garcia da. Colloquies on the Simples & Drugs of India, tr. Clements Markham. London: Henry Sotheran and Co., 1913 AO, pp. x-xi for a partial translation.

it among those who use it .... The men who eat it go about sleepily, and they say that they take it so as not to feel any trouble.

...

RUANO

How many kinds are there?

ORTA

There are many forms of it, different in the various lands. In Cairo (where they call it MECERI [Misree, from Misr, the Arabic name for Egypt, today the Janhuriyah Misr al-Arabiyah, or the Arab Republic of Egypt]) it is white and fetches a high price, and may be what we call TEBAICO [from Thebes]. At Aden [the Yemen] and various neighbouring places in the Red Sea it is black and very hard, the price varying. In Cambaya [Cambay, present day Khambhat, Gujurat], Mandou [Mandu, southwest central India], and Chitor [Chitoor, both a city and district in Andhra Pradesh] it is softer and more of a yellowing colour, and is worth more in many lands, because it is customary to eat it there, so that is is worth more in the countries where it is more used. I say this of Cambaya opium, as I called it, most of which comes from a country called Malvi [Mandavgod, on the Malwa plateau, Madhya Pradesh in central India].[12]

A little afterwards the Spanish botanist and physician Nicolás Bautista Monardes y Alfaro (c. 1493 – 1588) published in 1574 his *Primera y Segvnda y Tercera Partes de la Historia Medicinal, De las cosas que se traen de las Indias Occidentales,* which reiterated the information of Tomé Pirez and Garcia da Orta, mentioning with some admiration that the Asiatics are able to use up to sixty grains a day of *aphion* for rest and health:

---

[12] Orta, 1913, Forty-first Colloquy, pp. 330, 332-333; Orta, Garcia da. *Coloquios dos Simples & Drogas da India,* vol. II. Lisboa: Imprensa Nacional, 1892 AO, *Coloquio Quadragesimo Primeiro, Do Amfiam,* pp. 171, 173: *Queria saber a certeza do amfiam ... que chaman Malvi.*

This *Aphion* the Turkes doe ufe for this effecte. The Souldiers and Captaines that goe to Warres, when they labour much, after the time that they be lodged, that they may take their reft, they receiue *Aphion*, and fleepe with it, and remaine lightened of their labour. And furely it is a thing of admiration, to fee howe thefe Barbarous people doe take fuch Medicines, and how many of them doe take them, and they dos not kill them, but rather they take them for health and remedie for their neceffities. ... And truely it is a thing worthy of greate confideration, that fiue graines of *Opio* do kill us, and threefcore [60] doe giue them health and reft.[13]

These studies culminate with the *Tractado de las Drogas y medicinas de las Indias Orientales*, published in Burgos in 1578 by the Portuguese physician and natural historian Cristóbal Acosta (c. 1525 – 1594). To Acosta we are owed one of the first descriptions of the opium habit, which for this reason alone merits a mention. Not very accustomed to the prescribing of opium (a thing common among European doctors then), a little after arriving in India he was surprised to find the natives using opium is such large amounts without it affecting their ability to carry out their duties: "Ordinarily, they take every day from twenty grains to a drachma of opium. [But] I knew in Malabar .. the secretary to a judge of the king, very discreet and lively and with great ability and astuteness ... who ate every day the weight of five drachmas ...."[14]

---

[13] Monardes, Nicolas. Joyfull Newes Out of the New-found Worlde, Englished by John Frampton. London: Printed by E. Allde, by the afsigne of Bonhams Norton, 1596 AO, The Second Part of the thinges that are brought from the Weft Indias, Of the Tobaco, and of his great vertues, fol. 41; *Defte Aphio ufan los Turcos para efte efecto. Los Soldados ... que cinco granos di Opio nos maten, y feffenta les den a ellos falud y defcanso* (Monardes, Nicolas. *Primera y Segvnda y Tercera Partes de la Historia Medicinal, De las cosas que se traen de las Indias Occidentales*. Sevilla: En cafa de alonfo Efcriuano, 1574 AO, *Segvnda Parte del Libro, de las cofas que fe traen de nueftros Indias Occidentales, que firue al ufo de medicina, Del Tabaco y de svs grandes virtudes*, ff. 49-50).
[14] *El ordinario vfo que tienen de tomar cada dia del Opio, es de veynte granos ... que comia cada dia*

Besides recording the strength of the habit and the dangers of going cold turkey, he also seems to be the first to have effected a detoxification of some prisoners by a partial drug substitution:

One cannot leave the habit without great risk of life: which they would lose if they lacked opium, if with good pure wine, in place of opium we did not aid them. As it happened I knew a discreet and wise Turk in his own way, a natural of Aden, who (while I was sailing in the Indian Ocean toward the Cape of Good Hope in a ship, in which the poor Turk, with other Turks and Persians and Arabs who were captives of Portugal, had there some opium they had hidden to sustain themselves, taking a little as a medicine) told me that if he was not given opium he would not live two days. Being that in that ship I was in charge of curing the sick and caring for the poor, I ordered that each man habituated to opium each morning be given a swig of pure wine. And none of them died, and before a month was out they no longer wanted opium and it did them no harm the lack of it. And using sometimes the wine, along with a little opium that I had in the ship's stores, which I had brought along to cure the sick, neither opium nor wine did they wish.[15]

The anecdote highlights the lack of pharmacological knowledge regarding opium [and of how much of it the prisoners may have hidden away] on the part of Acosta with the picaresque of *vn difcreto y fabio Turco a fu guifa* (a discreet and wise Turk in his own way), but especially with the innocuousness of the feared abstinence syndrome. The *grãde riefgo de la vida* (great risk of life) evaporates like smoke, leaving behind the astonishment of Europeans confronted with the massive use of a drug which, as Garcia da Orta explained, permits one

---

pefo de cinco dragmas (Acosta, Cristóbal. <u>*Tractado de las Drogas, y medicinas de la Indias*</u> <u>*Orientales*</u>. Burgos: Por Martin de Victoria, 1578 Real Jardín Botanico, Biblioteca Digital, Madrid CSIC, bibdigital.rjb.csic.es, *Libro, qve trata de las Drogas medicinales, y de fus prouechos, cap. 68 Del Opio*, p. 415).

[15] *no le puedē dexar, fin grãde riefgo de la vida ... ni Opio ni vino quifieron* (Acosta, 1578, pp. 412-414).

of its most inveterate users *falava como homem letrado e discreto* (to speak like a discreet and educated man).[16]

2.   The Situation in the East.   The same does not happen with alcohol of course. But opium is still a subject carrying the inquisitional stigma. It is used as an anesthetic and for exceptional pain in Europe, while the *Asiatics* use it as a general euphoriant and seem immune to any undesirable effects. This is scandalous, even more so coming from peoples which are deprecated as infidels.

The distinction can be observed, for example, when in 1553 the French naturalist Pierre Belon du Mans (1517 – 1564) observed that the white poppy was cultivated abundantly in all of Cappadocia, Paphlagonia and Sicily, that opium was a product so greatly esteemed that there was no Turk who did not purchase it and if he were down to his last *asper*, he would spend half of it on opium, carrying it with him always, in times of peace and in times of war.[17] But in the nuance of spending down to his last *asper* there already appears a double reproach (to the user as prodigal and to the drug as enslaver) neither of which appears in the Arab literature. Opium is consumed from Alexandria to Beijing in a manner very analogous to the way alcohol is consumed in Europe. If an Arab were to say that no European could quit using wine even to the point of spending half of the last of his money on it, he would justly be accused of exaggeration.

---

[16] Orta, 1892, vol. II, *Coloquio Quadragesimo Primeiro, Do Amfiam*, p. 175; Orta, 1913, Forty-first Colloquy, Opium, p. 334.

[17] *Paphlagonie, Cappadoce, & Cilicie. Ilz sement les champs de Pauot blanc .... Il n'y a Turc qui n'en achete: & n'eut il vaillant qu'vn afpre, il en mettra la moitié en Opium, & le portera toufiours auec foy, tant en temps de paix qu'en guerre* (Pierre Belon du Mans. <u>Les Observations de Plvsievrs Singvlaritez et Choses Memorables</u>. Paris: Chez Hierofme de Marnef, 1588 AO, Book III, ch. XV, *Chofe digne de grande admiration des Turcs, qui mangent l'Opium, pour se rendre plus hardis à la guerre*, p. 404).

Around the same time as Belon's book appears, _De Medicina Aegyptorum_ is published by the Italian physician and botanist Prospero Alpini (1553 – 1617). He repeats the trope of Egyptians using opium to increase their sexual appetite.[18] He decries their _servitude de l'opium_ (enslavement to opium) and detoxes some of them with _vin vieux_ (old wine) boiled with _gingembre et d'autres condiments_ (ginger and other spices) taken _quatre fois par jour_ (four times a day).[19] On the one hand he admits that some Egyptians take the drug _pendent soixante ans, en absorbent jusqu'à deux drachmes par jour_ (for sixty years, absorbing up to two drachmas a day).[20] But on the other he quickly lists their symptoms, from consumption, bad digestion, somnolence, memory loss, and constipation.[21]

This alcohol-philic viewpoint on drugs will continue well into the nineteenth century. The Hungarian traveler Ármin Vámbéry (1832 – 1913) writes: "Thus, for instance, the prohibition of wine and tobacco led to the enjoyment of the much more injurious opium."[22] Otherwise, he has nothing good to say about opium, or about cannabis either, repeatedly disparaging both customs:

[T]his man was a tiryaki (opium-eater), a scapegrace, who I should, as much as possible, avoid. ... [T]he crazy opium-eater .... [U]ntil he had given up his vicious habit of opium-eating .... [T]wo half-naked dervishes on the point of swallowing down their noonday dose of opium .... They then prepared tea for me, and while I

---

[18] _aux Égyptiens pour augmenter l'appétit sexuel_ (Alpini, Prospero. _Histoire naturelle de l'Égypte_, tr. R. de Fenoyl. Caire: Institut français d'archéologie orientale du Caire, 1979 AO, Ch. XI, p. 263).

[19] Alpini, 1979, p. 263.

[20] Alpini, 1979, p. 257.

[21] Alpini, 1979, p. 257.

[22] Vámbéry, Arminius. History of Bokhara, 2nd ed. London: Henry S. King & Co., 1873 AO, ch. XVII, pp. 363-364.

drank it they took their own poisonous opiate, and in half an hour were in the happy realms; then, although I saw in the features of one slumberer traces of internal gladness, I detected in those of the other convulsive movements, picturing the agony of death. ... I found here several dervishes, who had become as thin as skeletons by the fatal indulgence in that opium called beng (prepared from flax) ....[23]

But the sixteenth century is the point of inflection in the Western attitude toward the juice of the poppy. Thus one observes continually this mix of interest and rejection. Only somewhat later, when the drug will become in Europe a therapeutic panacea once again, will we encounter objective testimony, coinciding with the Arabic tradition.

Looking ahead to the nineteenth century Chinese opium wars, this may be a good moment to put to rest a popular myth regarding opium, that the strength of the opium imported into China in the nineteenth century was the cause of their so-called *opium problem*. Opium varies widely in its morphine content depending on the variety, where and how it has been grown and processed, the season and even from capsule to capsule on the same plant, making all such comparisons problematic. Further, it varies widely by region as well:

The Smyrna opium is generally considered the best in the European market, but even in this the morphia varies between four and fourteen percent. ... Generally, also the Indian and Persian samples yield less morphia than those of Turkey. ... British-grown opium contains more morphia than that of commerce [and some report] the presence of 16 to 28 percent of morphia in some opium collected in France.[24]

---

[23] Vámbéry, Ármin. Travels in Central Asia. NY: Harper & Brothers, 1865 AO, pp. 52, 113, 114, 179, 183.

[24] "The Narcotics we indulge in – Part II," *Blackwood's Edinburgh Magazine*, vol. LSSIV, July-Dec 1853 (American edition, vol. XXXVII). NY: Leonard Scot and Company, 1853, p. 613 (GB).

Thus China generally received weaker (measured in morphine content) opium from India while Europeans imported a stronger product from Turkey, Britain and France:

Most of the imported paste from India and the locally cultivated opium in China had a very low morphine content, on average 3 or 4%. On the other hand, the opium imported every year into nineteenth-century England from Turkey in the thousands of tonnes was very rich in morphine, ranging from 10 to 15%. Furthermore, smoking was generally acknowledged to be more wasteful than ingestion .... [Eighty to ninety percent] of the active compound was lost from fumes which either escaped from the pipe or were exhaled by the smoker.[25]

[This difference in morphine as well as habituation may account for the European observations of the large quantities used in Asia.]

But quality was not necessarily correlated with strength. Lin Zexu, the Chinese mandarin who seized the British opium at Canton in 1839, carefully opened and examined the chests. He then organized the product by quality and origin:

[We] arrive at the colors and names of the opium. There are also differences. The black is called *Gōng Bān* [evenly colored] *Tǔ* [opium]. I hear it is the highest grade of opium. *Bái* [white] *Tǔ* is next in sequence. *Jīn Huā* [Gold Flower] *Tǔ* in addition is next in sequence. Splitting open the chests to melt and transform. We manage all kinds of opium. Separately we number and register [them]. Generally speaking *Gōng Tǔ* and *Bái Tǔ* make up the majority. *Jīn Huā Tǔ* falls short of one percent [tr. gwr].[26]

P. C. Kuo, who first partially translated Lin's memorials to the emperor in 1935, added in brackets the locations where the opium had been grown: "There are different kinds of opium. The black opium is

---

[25] Dikotter, 2016, opendemocracy.net.
[26] Robinette, Glenn. Did Lin Zexu Make Morphine? vol. III. Valparaiso, Chile: Graffiti Militante Press, 2020, p. 73.

called *Kung pan tou* [Patna], said to be the best. Next to it is *Pak tou* [Malwa]. Still inferior is *Chin hwa tou* [Persian]."[27]

Both Patna and Malwa were sold by brokers in Calcutta and Bombay, respectively. If the percentage of morphine from 1853 was similar to the opium of 1839, then Chinese conoisseurs preferred a weaker product to the relatively stronger one from Persia. Those readers familiar with alcohol are well aware that the quality of wine is generally independent of its percentage of alcohol. So yes, the opium from Europe and Turkey was stronger but no, very little of it nor the Persian ever reached China, and the Chinese smoker preferred the opium from India anyway.

Those who would blame the strength of the opium imported into China for China's so-called *opium problem* in the nineteenth century must explain why nineteenth century Europeans (who enjoyed a free trade in the drug) seemed to have had no problem with a stronger product while nineteenth century Chinese (who endured a national prohibition) suffered from a weaker one. A sixteenth century European traveler voices astonishment at the quantities ingested without harm in the East. A nineteenth century Chinese might have been just as surprised at the massive quantities of strong opium imported into and grown domestically in Europe.

---

[27] Robinette, 2008, vol. II, p. 281; Kuo, P. C. A Critical Study of the First Anglo-Chinese War with Documents. Taipei: Ch'eng Wen Publishing Co., 1970 (1935), pp. 243-247; compare Orta's descriptions from centuries earlier (Orta, 1913, Forty-first Colloquy, pp. 330, 332-333; Orta, 1892, pp. 171, 173: *Queria saber a certeza do amfiam ... que chaman Malvi*).

Figure 122. *Der Apoteker* (The Apothecary), woodcut by Swiss-German artist Jost
Amman (1539 – 1591), from *Eygentlich Befchreibung Aller Stande Auff Erden*
(The Book of Trades). Franckfurt am Mayn: Feyerbents, 1568
digital.slub-dresden.de, p. 18, text by Hans Sachs.

C.   The Recuperation of Opium

Paracelsus and his disciples demonstrated the possibility of employing great quantities of good opium as an anesthetic in surgery, while blazing a trail toward diverse opiate preparations very different in purpose and composition to the ancient triacas. Now poppy juice was mixed with expensive substances like saffron, gold powders, amber, jade, pearls, precipitates of precious stones, and so forth, in agreement with the original alchemical theory that satisfied various exigencies at the same time. On the one hand the client saw his symptoms alleviated thanks to the intense sedative, analgesic and astringent action of the drug, and on the other the doctor had motives for asking exorbitant fees; moreover, this ensured that the availability of what had been formerly the shit of the devil remained restricted to the upper classes, as an exceptional and new medicine.

In a certain way it resurrected the GrecoRoman distinction of one medicine for the rich and another for the poor. That of the latter still made use often enough of the medieval recipes of white witchcraft (holy water, masses, candles, etc.) or black (unguents often composed of the solanaceas), while the new therapy for the rich rarely excluded the combination of opium and noble materials. The European literature of the period (from Shakespeare to Cervantes, and from Lope de Vega[28] to Molière) contains occasional references to preparations of this type, never lacking in sarcasm over the vanity of the patients and the rapacity of their therapists.

1.   The Investigations in the Low Countries.   From the middle of the seventeenth century, the Dutch control the way stations that make possible the spice route from the East Indies. In order to

---

[28] Spanish playwright and poet Lope Félix de Vega Carpio (1562 – 1635).

maintain this commerce they employ the system already put in place by the Lusitanians [Portuguese] which was, in part, to use the opium from Asia Minor as a trade good. This assured a wide availability of the drug in their cities, as well as among its proponents including physiologists and clinicians who have passed on into universal history.

The first of these was the Flemish natural philosopher J. B. van Helmont (1580 – 1644), founder of iatrochemistry which uses "chemical concepts to explain physiological and pathological phenomena."[29] Besides demonstrating the presence of what he called the *gas sylvester* (carbon dioxide, named *gas* from the Greek *chaos* and *sylvestris*, meaning, from the wood), he became known (along with many other physicians who prescribed opium) as *Doctor Opiatus* for his admiration for the substance. From one contemporary perspective his writings show the "intimate blending of the practical and mystical. ... [H]e represents the transition from alchemy to chemistry, and is a worthy predecessor of Boyle, who studied him carefully and adapted many of his ideas."[30] Van Helmont pointed out the inconsistencies in the traditional classification of opium: "They declare in *Opium*, a heightened cold to be, and alfo a heat in its bitterneffe: And fo alfo, I have now rendred their knowledge drawn from favours, ridiculous, from one only example ...."[31]

Another follower of Van Helmont and Paracelsus, the physician Thomas Willis (1621 – 1675) adopted a more practical, even-handed approach. On the one hand, "*Opium* is efteemed of moft

---

[29] Parent, André. "Franciscus Sylvius on Clinical Teaching, Iatrochemistry and Brain Anatomy," *The Cambridge Journal of Neurological Sciences*, 2016, p. 598, cambridge.org.

[30] Partington, J. R. "Joan Baptista van Helmont," *Annals of Science*, vol. I, no. 4, 15 Oct 1936, pp. 359, 385.

[31] Helmont, John Baftifa Van. Oriatrike, or Phyfick Refined, tr. John Chandler. London: Printed for Lodowick Loyd, 1662 AO, ch. XXIII, Nature is ignorant of contraries, p. 169.

excellent ufe for the quieting of all manner of Pains whatfoever, wherefore it defervedly is wont to be called *Nepenthe*, and is a truly divine Remedie. ... The Dyfenterick Affections can fcarce be cured without *Opium*."[32] On the other hand, he felt compelled to point out "as we have declared its benefits, fo it behooves us to admonish you of its harms."[33] He railed against those doctors who, prescribing "too great or untimely a Dofe of it have snatched away their [patients'] lives," calling them "Quackfalvers and Empiricks."[34] Like Da Orta and Acosta, he notes that the Turks seem immune to such problems despite a relatively heavy use of the substance, which he attributes to their becoming accustomed to the drug: "But that *Opium* is devoured in a great quantity by the Turks ... unhurt, or at leaft without any danger of life; the Reafon is ... by the frequent ufe they at length become more congruous and familiar."[35]

---

[32] Willis, Thomas. <u>Pharmaceutice Rationalis: or, an Exercitation of the Operations of Medicine in Humane Bodies</u>, Part One. London: Printed for T. Dring, C. Harper, and F. Leigh, 1679 AO, Section VII, Ch. I, Of Opiate Medicines or Caufing Sleep (retitled The Good Effects of Opium as a page heading), pp. 140, 142; *Opium pro doloribus ... remedium vere divinum exiftit. ... Affectus Dyfenterici fine Opio vix curari poffunt* (Willis, Thomas. <u>Pharmaceutice Rationalis sive Diatriba de Medicamentorum Operationibus in Humano Corpore</u>, third edition. Oxoniae: E. Theatro Sheldoniano, 1679 AO, part 1, sect. VII, cap. I, *De Medicamentis Opiatis, five fomnum inducentibus*, retitled *Opiatarum effectus Boni*, pp. 146, 149).

[33] Willis, 1679, Section VII, Ch. 2, Of the Harms and Incommodities of Opium, to which is added Cautions about the use of it (retitled The Harms of Opium as a page heading), p. 144; *quare prout commodorum, ita & noxarum ejus admoneri nos oportet* (Willis, 1679, Sectio VII, cap. II, *De Opii nocumentis, ac incommodis; quibus fubnectuntur cautiones circa ufum ejus*, retitled *Opii nocumenta*, p. 151).

[34] Willis, 1679, Section VII, ch. 2, p. 144; *aut intempeftivam ejus dofin, aut vitam fuam corripuere* (Willis, 1679, Sectio VII, Cap. II, p. 151).

[35] Willis, 1679, Section VII, ch. 2, p. 145; *Quod vero opium à Turcis ... & familiares evadunt* (Willis, 1679, Sectio VII, Cap. II, p. 152).

Willis was also one of the first to describe an experiment that transfused opium into the veins of an animal:

Many years ago we faw about three ounces of the tincture of *Opium* done in Canary [wine] transfufed into the Jugulary Vein of a little Dog, the vein being clofed the dog ran about after his wonted manner and feemed little or nothing affected or changed; after a quarter of an hour he began to be a little ftupefied, to nod his head, and at length began to foll into a Sleep, but not permitting him when we had hindred him a while by beating, terrifying, and courfing him about, at length the foporous Affection being fo done away he became whole and lively enough ....[36]

Perhaps the most important follower of van Helmont was the German physician, anatomist (who named a fissure in the brain), and chemist Franz de le Boë (Franciscus Sylvius, 1614 – 1672), a professor of medicine at the University of Leiden known habitually as Sylvius (latinized, de le Boë is literally, of the woods). He became one of the most influential pedagogues and investigators of the century, who consolidated the viewpoint of his master and the thesis that all the vital and pathological phenomenon are the product of chemical actions. As doctors and students from all over Europe attended his classes, he was an even more effective propagandist for the opiates than his teachers, even prescribing them in certain cases for snake bite in children:

If *the Jaundice* be caused *by the bite of a Viper*, or any other Creature, we must ... *both amend, and again expel that Poison.* To which purpose sundry *Opiats* are used, as, *Treacle, Mithridate, Diascordium,* &c. Which by the Opium and other things wherewith they

---

[36] Willis, 1679, Section VII, ch. 3, The Kinds, Preparations, and Forms of Opiates, pp. 149-150; *Ante multos annos Opii tincturae, in vino Canarino ... demum affectione foporofa ita prorfus abacta fotis fanus, & vegetus evafit* (Willis, 1679, Sectio VII, Cap. III, *Opiatarum fpecies, preparationes, & formulae*, p. 157).

abound, do not only amend the spirituous volatility of Vipers Poyson; but moreover by their many sweating ingredients expel the same through the Pores of the Skin ....[37]

Works (especially the animal experiments) by Samuel Schröer (1675 – 1732)[38] and the Virginian physician and legislator John Leigh (c. 1755 – 1796)[39] can be derived from Boë, written within a current that transcended the iatrochemical school but continued to be focused on the drug.[40]

This tradition was continued by another clinician and professor from Leiden, the physician, chemist and botanist Herman Boerhaave (1668 – 1738), who pioneered a quantitative approach, introduced bedside, clinical teaching and named the Boerhaave Syndrome (spontaneous esophageal rupture). Thanks to him the Faculty of Medicine at said university was converted into one of the most prestigious teaching centers in Europe since the disciples of Boerhaave would occupy for generations the professorships at Edinburgh and Vienna, as well as various German cities: "As a master of bedside teaching Boerhaave can be regarded as the originator of modern

---

[37] Boë, Frans de le. Of Childrens Diseases, given in a familiar style for weaker capacities, tr. Richard Gower. London: George Downs, 1682 (Early English Books Online, hereinafter EEBO), ch. 1, Of the Jaundice, pp. 26-27; *Quòd fi à Viperae ... idem per cutis poros expellere* (Deleboe, Francisci, Sylvii. *Opera Medica*. Amstelodami: Apud Danielem Elsevirium et Abrahamum Wolfgang, 1679 AO, *Praxeos Medicae Appendix, Tractatus I, De Morbis Infantum, cap. I, De Ictero*, LXXXVI-LXXXVII, p. 595).

[38] *De Opii natura et usu* (1693), his university thesis.

[39] "An Experimental Inquiry into the Properties of Opium and its Effects on Living Subjects," for which he won the Harveian Prize at Edinburgh.

[40] See also for example *Opiologia* (1618) by Angelus Sala Vincentius, the *Pharmacopoea universa medicamenta* (1622) of Juan del Castillo, *De opio tractatus* (1635) by Daniel Winckler, the *Dissertatio medica de chiurgia infusoria* (1668) of Georg Frederich Stirius, and *Opiologia* (1739) by Georg Wolfgang Wedel.

medical education. Huge numbers of foreign students went to Leiden to learn from him ...."[41]

Like van Helmont and Sylvius, Boerhaave considered opium "one of the moft powerful Drugs we know. It is the greateft of all Anodynes; and it brings on Sleep with certainty. It is alfo a high Cordial, a Sudorific, and an Aftringent. All thefe Qualities it poffeffes in a great Degree; its Value therefore is obvious."[42] But he was not unmindful of its potential harms: "If the Pains or Convulfions be very urgent [in nephritis], without waiting for the Effects of other Remedies, give Opiates with due Caution. ... Opiates ought feldom and not but with the greateft prudence to made ufe of."[43] A colleague at the same university, the chemist Jacob Le Mort (1650 – 1718) is credited (probably incorrectly) with the invention of the Elixir Asthmaticum which

became official in the London Pharmacopoeia of 1721. ... In the London Pharmacopoeia of 1746, the name was changed to Elixir Paregoricum, which is still used as a synonym for paregoric. Later, the preparation became Tincturata Opii Camphorata in the Edinburgh, Dublin and U. S. Pharmacopoeias .... The evidence does not seem to justify his being credited with the discovery or origination of paregoric.[44]

---

[41] Hull, Gillian. "The Influence of Herman Boerhaave," *Journal of the Royal Society of Medicine*, vol. 90, September 1997, p. 512.

[42] Goade, Richard, tr., ed. Herman Boerhaave's Materia Medica, or the Druggists' Guide. London: Printed for the Author, 1755 AO, p. 205.

[43] Delacoste, J., ed. Boerhaave's Aphorisms: Concerning the Knowledge and Cure of Diseases. London: Printed for B. Cowfe, and W. Innys, 1715 AO, numbers 998, 1357, pp. 262, 371.

[44] Boyd, Eldon M. and Marion L. MacLachlan. "The Expectorant Action of Paregoric," *Canadian Medical Association Journal*, vol. 50, no. 4, April 1944, pp. 339-340, ncbi.nlm.nih.gov.

CH. 13 THE TRANSITION TOWARD MODERNITY

The original formula for the Elixir Paregoricum follows: "Take flowers of Benjamin, opium ftrained, of each a dram; of camphire two fcruples; of the effential oil of anisfeeds half a dram; of rectified fpirit of wine a quart. After digeftion ftrain off the fpirit."[45]   The opium, camphor and alcohol in the compound remain in the paregoric still prescribed (rarely) today in the US, and lost in the backrooms of some present-day pharmacies in Spain.

It should not be forgotten that the seventeenth century is the moment of maximum political and cultural apogee for the Low Countries. A not depreciable part of their returns were then coming from the Dutch East India Company (which imported spices and exported opium) and from the Dutch West India Company (whose principal source of income was the traffic in slaves from Africa to America). This apogee, together with the complex European political situation, is the cause of successive wars with the English (triggered by the Navigation Act of 1651[46] which prohibited foreign ships from intervening in any commercial British transaction on the continent or overseas) and which will result in severe reverses for the exterior commerce of the small country. Holland lost its enclaves in North America and had to accept conditions that limited its former control of

---

[45] Pemberton, H., tr. The Dispensatory of the Royal College of Phyficians, London. London: Printed for T. Longman and T. Shewell ... and J. Nourse, 1746 AO, p. 283.
[46] Firth, C. W. and R. S. Rait, eds. Acts and Ordinances of the Interregnum 1642 – 1660, vol. II. London: Published by His Majesty's Stationery Office, 1911 (babel.hathitrust.org, hereinafter BHO), p. 559: "An Act for the increase of Shipping, and Encouragement of the Navigation of this Nation [9 October 1651]: ... no Goods or Commodities whatsoever, of the Growth, Production or Manufacture of Asia, Africa or America, or of any part thereof ... shall be Imported or brought into this Commonwealth of England ... in any Ship or Ships, Vessel or Vessels whatsoever, but onely in such as do truly and without fraud belong onely to the People of this Commonwealth ... as the Proprietors or right Owners thereof."

the seas. For the events of our history, it is striking the coincidence of the Dutch colonial enterprise with the therapeutic enthroning of opium, since something very similar had been told during the sixteenth century with Portugal. One could say that he who traffics in poppy juice becomes fascinated by its virtues, as will confirm the clinical movement favorable to the drug which surges in England from the middle of the seventeenth century, when this country begins to assume a larger and larger part of the commerce in the drug to the Far East.

It's worthwhile to observe that this occurs (beginning with Paracelsus) chiefly in the zones where church reformation has triumphed, whose tribunals against witchcraft are the first to exclude opium from the list of theologically suspect substances, while in Portugal, Spain and France, the unconditional acceptance of the drug happens somewhat later. On the other hand, its principal supporters in Holland and England (as later in France) are religious devotees, the Capuchin monk van Helmont and Lutheran pastor Boerhaave, who before embracing medical careers and throughout all their lives maintained postures of rigorous piety and orthodoxy within their respective churches.

Opium appears to them as a divine gift, a balm to endure any kind of suffering, which previous therapies could not alleviate in the same degree. Like the great Muslim physicians Avicenna, Rhazes, and Avempace, these European physicians and clinicians take it for an unequalled gift among the recourses of the pharmacopoeia. At the same time they counsel moderation and even abstinence both with it and with the other traditional drugs (alcohol, the solanaceas), as well as with the new (tobacco and coffee).

2.   The Attitude in England and France.   The   physician Thomas Sydenham (1624 – 1689), known as the English Hippocrates, who lent his name to Sydenham's chorea (St. Vitus' Dance), experimented with cinchona bark on fevers, and may well be responsible for the warning to all medical students, *Primum non nocere*, also put into circulation the laudanum named for him. As to the spread and permanence of the preparation one need only say, for example, that in Spain it was until 1977 still listed as one of the medicines in stock at the Office of the Pharmacy. The formula for Paracelsian laudanum is lost in the mists of time and seventeenth century medicine already knew of a tincture (the laudanum of another Swiss, Theodor Zwinger the Elder (1533- 1588). But only the *vinum opii* of Sydenham achieved general acceptance. This physician is said to have personally prescribed, according to his own testimony, some eight thousand *litres* of his laudanum to illustrious contemporaries like Oliver Cromwell (1599 – 1658) and Charles II (1630 – 1685) among others. Supposedly, he himself took daily twenty grams of the preparation, whose formula follows:

14. The liquid laudanum, which I conftantly ufe, as above intimated, is prepared in the following fimple manner: *Take of* Spanish *wine, one pint; opium, two ounces; faffron, one ounce; cinnamon and cloves reduced to powder, of each one dram; infufe them together in a bath-heat for two or three days, till the tincture becomes of a due confiftence, and after ftraining it off, fet it by for ufe.*[47]

Sydenham used to say that his drugs would fit in the pommel of his cane, three quarters of it already occupied by opium, so it has been reported. He considered it "a most excellent cardiac, not to say

---

[47] Sydenham, Thomas. The Entire Works of Dr Thomas Sydenham, tr. John Swain. London: Printed by R. Cave, 1763 AO, Section 4, Chapter III, The Dyfentery of part of 1669, and of 1670, 1671, 1672, p. 161; see also, Sydenham, Thomas. The Works of Thomas Sydenham, M. D. on Acute and Chronic Diseases, ed. Benjamin Rush. Philadelphia: E. Kimber et al, 1815 AO, The Dysentery of Part of 1669, and of 1670, 1671, 1672, section 14, p. 155.

the only one hitherto discovered."[48] His illustrious colleagues in the Low Countries would certainly have been in agreement with his high opinion of the drug:

And here I cannot help mentioning with gratitude the goodness of the Supreme Being, who has supplied afflicted mankind with opiates for their relief: no other remedy being equally powerful to overcome a great number of diseases, or to eradicate them effectually. ... Moreover, this medicine is so necessary an instrument in the hands of a skilful person, that the art of physic would be defective and imperfect without it; and whoever is thoroughly acquainted with its virtues, and the manner of using it, will perform greater things than might reasonably be expected from the use of any single medicine.[49]

Almost as celebrated as Sydenham (though not so notable a physician) was Thomas Dover (1660 – 1742). After finishing his studies he acted as a privateer for many years in the Americas, with quite a success. He sacked the coast of Peru commanding four ships, satisfactorily treated the plague loosed upon that littoral with opium and, to finish, when returning with an immense fortune, rescued Alexander Selkirk (the Robinson Crusoe of Daniel Defoe) from the islands of Juan Fernández. Even before enriching himself, while working as an internist in Bristol, Dover was one of the first doctors who offered free therapy to the poor.

Upon his return from so many vicissitudes, he established an original consult in the Jerusalem Coffee House in London and sold the powders under his name, also called *diaphoretics*, whose formula made him a millionaire, combining opium with *ipecacuana*, a plant emetic, tonic, purgative and sudorific, especially effective against amoebic dysentery. Dover's powders were sold in drugstores like aspirin or

---

[48] Sydenham, 1815, p. 156.
[49] Sydenham, 1815, p. 155.

bicarbonate soda is sold today, although for a much wider range of symptoms, from general pain to insomnia, from uterus contractions to gastric illnesses. It was the first cheap opiate medicine, the first not linked to a pharmacopoeia restricted to the rich. His formula is as follows:

Take Opium one Ounce, Salt-Petre and Tartar vitriolated, each four Ounces, Ipocacuana one Ounce, Liquorifh one Ounce. Put the Salt-Petre and Tartar into a red-hot Mortar, ftirring them with a Spoon till they have done flaming. Then powder them very fine; after that flice in your Opium; grind thefe to a Powder, and then mix the other Powders with thefe. Dofe from forty to fixty or feventy Grains in a Glafs of White-Wine Poffet, going to bed. Covering up warm, and drinking a Quart or three Pints of the Poffet-Drink while fweating.[50]

With Sydenham, Dover and their disciples, England became the center of experimentation with opium injected intravenously. The originator was the architect, anatomist and physicist Sir Christopher Wren (1632 – 1723), one of the most celebrated personalities of the century.[51] At Oxford in 1656 Wren injected into the vein of a dog a dose of opium.

The famous experiment took place in the chambers of the honorable Robert Boyle (1627 – 1691), the Anglo-Irish founder of modern chemistry, founder and fellow of the Royal Society, responsible for Boyle's Law, who narrates:

---

[50] Dover, Thomas. The Ancient Physician's Legacy to his Country. London: Printed for the Author, 1732 wellcomelibary.org, Gout, or Arthritis, pp. 18-19.

[51] Professor of astronomy at Oxford, founder and president of the Royal Society, the finest English architect of his time, to whom we owe Trinity College in Cambridge, Chelsea Hospital and Saint Paul's Cathedral in London, among many other monuments.

His [Wren's] way (which is much better learn'd by fight, then relation) was briefly this: First, to make a fmall and opportune Incifion over that part of the hind leg, where the larger Veffels that carry the Blood, are moft eafie to be taken hold of: Then to make a Ligarture upon thofe Veffels, and to apply a certain fmall Plate of Brafs (of above half an Inch long, and about a quarter of an Inch broad, whofe fides were bending inwards) almoft of the fhape and bignefs of the Nail of a Mans thumb, but fomewhat longer. ... This Plate being well faften'd on, he made a Slit along the Vein, from the Ligature towards the Heart, great enough to put in at it the flender Pipe of a Syringe: By which I had propof'd to have injected a warm folution of *Opium* in Sack [wine], that the effect of our Experiment might be the more quick and manifeft. And accordingly our dexterous Experimenter ... convey'd a fmall Dofe of the Solution or Tincture into the open'd Veffel, whereby, getting into the mafs of Blood ... it was quickly, by the circular motion of That, carry'd to the Brain, and other parts of the body. So that we had fcarce unty'd the Dog ... before the *Opium* began to difclofe its Narcotick Quality, and almoft affoon as he was upon his feet, he began to nod with his head, and faulter and reel in his pace, and prefently after appear'd fo ftupifi'd, that there were Wagers offer'd his Life could not be fav'd. But I ... cauf'd him to be whipp'd up and down the Neighboring Garden, whereby being kept awake, and in motion, after some time he began to come to himfelf again; and being led home, and carefully tended [he grew] fat fo manifeftly that 'twas admir'd.[52]

Boyle was no stranger to the benefits and dangers of prescribing opium:

That Opium is reckon'd by Phyfitians among Poifons, I need not tell you; and yet fuch powerful Remedies may be made with it for many defperate Cafes, efpecially in hot Countries, that the good it may doe, fo much exceeds the harm, that Phyfitians would be forry there were none of it in the World.[53]

---

[52] Boyle, Robert. <u>Some Considerations touching the Vsefvlnesse of Experimental Naturall Philofophy</u>. Oxford: Printed by Hen: Hall, 1663 AO, Poftfcript, Second Part, First Section, Essay II, pp. 62-63.
[53] Boyle, 1663, p. 48.

CH. 13 THE TRANSITION TOWARD MODERNITY

Some months later Wren attempted another experiment that did not turn out so well. Again, Boyle narrates:

And fome Moneths after a foreign Ambaffador ... did me the Honor to vifit me, and inform'd me, That he had cauf'd tryal to be made, with infufion of *Crocus Metallorum*, upon an inferior Domeftick of his that deferv'd to have been hangd; but that the fellow, as foon as ever the Injection began to be made, did (either really or craftily), fall into a Swoon; whereby, being unwilling to profecute fo hazardous an Experiment, they defifted, without feeing any other Effect of it.[54]

Wren had already verified that opium not only worked in a very different way in men than in animals but even from one species to another, since dogs could absorb large amounts but a cat fell into a delirium. According to Boyle:

[W]e have more than once given to a Dog, without much harming him, fuch a quantity of *Opium*, as would probably have fuffic'd to have kill'd feveral Men ... (as when lately a Cat ran mad, fo that her Keeper was fain to kill her) upon a large dofe of Opium which we caufed to be given her.[55]

Willis noticed the same phenomenon: "Dogs devour *Opium* in a great quantity without any fleepinefs or death. A little dofe of it prefently kils a Cat ...."[56]

In France, as noticed earlier, the movement in favor of opium therapy had its principal representative in the missionary and favorite diplomat of minister Jean-Baptiste Colbert (1619 – 1683), the Capuchin Henri Rousseau de Montbazon (Abbot Rousseau, 1643 – 1694), who prepared drugs for the poor as well. With opium eaters as

[54] Boyle, 1663, p. 64.
[55] Boyle, 1663, p. 57.
[56] Willis, 1679, Section VII, ch. 3, p. 149; *Canis Opium in quantitate magna* ... (Willis, 1679, Sectio VII, Cap. III, p. 157).

illustrious as Richelieu, Colbert and even Louis XIV, it is not strange that Rousseau would have a laboratory in the Louvre palace and receive an honorary doctorate from the Sorbonne as an award for his invention. This appears to have been due to specific recommendations from the Sun King. The formula for Rousseau's laudanum is as follows:

I take thus a pound of opium which I rub hard in a bowl of grease, where there are three pounds of common water; continuing like this until everything very much reduces to a sludge or silt with the water, which dissolves at the same time that which is dissolvable. Having fermented in my oven three pounds of honey with twelve pounds of water, I warm what is in my bowl and pour it into the vessel in which is my fermentation (this is a long-necked flask of glass set aside for this purpose) and that which is loamy does not dissolve at first; however, the action of fermentation resolves it and purifies it over time; and that excites a broth much stronger than honey alone. When the fermentation is finished, I distill the Eau-de-vie in a coolant; it smells like opium; and it can be used like this if one wants; because the anodine virtue of opium is in its oil alone. ... From which it happens that ten, fifteen, twenty, forty or fifty drops of this Eau-de-vie have an effect so sweet and so sure that I have never seen an accident [tr. gwr].[57]

Can we compare the strength of the laudanum in the recipes of Sydenham and Rousseau with that of the powders of Dover? But we have already seen that opium was not one thing but many things, varying depending on its source and how it was grown. Further, the timelines of these three physicians cover almost the entire seventeenth century and their geography much of Europe. Can we believe that the source material for their recipes was genuinely the same?

---

[57] *Je prend donc une livre d'Opium que je frote ... n'en voit jamais arriver aucun accident* (Rousseau, Abbé. *Secrets et Remedes Eprovez.* Paris: Chez Claude Jombert, 1718 AO, ch. V, *Diftinction de la Manipulation*, pp. 98-99).

Moreover, to compare accurately we would need the precise dose to be employed. But Sydenham does not give a specific dose for his laudanum and compares his own somewhat unfavorably in its *virtues* to other laudanums widely sold at the time:

I do not indeed judge that this preparation is to be preferred to the folid *laudanum* of the fhops on account of its virtues, but I gave it the preference for its more convenient form, and the greater certainty of dofing it, as it may be dropt into wine, a diftilled water, or any other liquor.[58]

Once prepared, his laudanum is then diluted in wine, water or liquor but there is no set quantity recommended. There is also the difference between his newly prepared and his older laudanum, observed by Swain in a footnote:

It is furprizing, that none of the pharmaceutical writers take any notice of the defects of *Sydenham's* liquid laudanum; yet it is certain that, after it has been kept for some time, about one fourth part of the opium contained in it is loft in a grofs fediment. This lofs is attended with great inconvenience; for during the precipitation, the laudanum is growing always weaker, fo that newly prepared laudanum, is, perhaps, a fourth part stronger than the fame laudanum when it has ftood for any time.[59]

Benjamin Rush, on the other hand, adds a note to the opposite effect: "The reader will perceive this tincture of opium to be stronger than the common laudanum of our shops, and attend to it in the prescriptions of that medicine by our author."[60] Swain also notices that there exists a different tincture of opium for which there are no objections to "the

---

[58] Sydenham, 1763, p. 162; Sydenham, 1815, p. 155.

[59] Sydenham, 1763, p. 161, note *(p)* by John Swain.

[60] Sydenham, 1815, p. 155, note (*) by Benjamin Rush.

uncertainty of the dofe; for in that, it is fo contrived as to be determined by weight."[61]

Similarly, we have seen that Rousseau recommends anywhere from ten to fifty drops as a dosage, a range of 500%, but he also clarifies that his dosages are not to be strictly adhered to: "Although I do not attach myself so scrupulously to giving it neither by weight nor measure, I have never seen an unfortuate accident."[62] Dover, on the other hand, rcommends a dose of from forty to seventy grains in a glass of white wine posset (a popular drink of milk, spices and often alcohol) but then suggests the patient drink from a quart to three pints of the posset afterwards.[63] One could add that neither weights nor measures had become standardized in this era.

In short, for too many reasons these three formulas are difficult to compare. The seventeenth century appears to a modern reader as a moment of experimentation and trial and error with regards to opiate medicines. Nor until Sertürner and the beginnings of analytic chemistry in the nineteenth century can one establish reasonably precise values for the percentage of morphine in a given sample. What is clear is that all three physicians, Sydenham, Dover and Rousseau, are not necessarily looking to create the strongest opiate remedy but rather the safest.

Consider that only a century earlier the humanists had talked in whispers of opium. Porta was charged for recommending its medical use, and those therapists not suspected of deviationism considered it a source of stupid dreams whose use only was called for in cases of really insufferable pain. In contrast, what the principal European medical

---

[61] Sydenham, 1763, p. 162, note *(p)* by John Swain.

[62] *Et quoique je ne m'attache par fi fcrupuleufement à le donner par poids ni par mefure; je n'en ai jamais vû aucun accident facheux* (Rousseau, 1718, p. 99).

[63] Dover, 1732, pp. 18-19.

authorities now thought is almost inexplicable without taking into account a change of attitude in the face of pain and the pharmacological modification of consciousness.

Simply, suffering did not now appear to be a gift from god, and the soft additional dreaming that opium produced did not incur the threat of the sin of apostasy. It is without doubt a great change, parallel to other great changes in European mentality. From the shit of the devil opium had come to be considered a divine gift. Between the two extremes, as a middle path, the colonial European enterprise began by converting the shit of the devil into the shit of the Muslims and other infidels, then proved opium's exceptional pharmacological virtues especially in Asia, and finished by converting Europe not only into the prime exporter, but also the prime world importer of the substance.

D.   The New Drugs

This peaceful agreement among therapists, the public and good customs with opium stands out for its absence with regards to other drugs when they began to penetrate into all corners of the globe.

1.   The Polemic Over Tobacco.   As previously noted, Spain was out front of other countries in fiscally taxing the importation of *Nicotiana tabacum* (L.) from its plantations in Hispañola and Cuba. Spain had no competition until 1610 when Captain John Rolfe (1585 – 1622), husband of the princess Pocahontas (daughter of the chief Powahatan), delayed by a shipwreck, finally managed to set foot in Jamestown. The colonists had tried cultivating the local variety, *Nicotiana rusticum*, but the result was, in the words of the first secretary to the Virginia colony, William Strachey (1572 – 1621), practically unsmokeable: "There is here great store of tobacco, which the salvages call apooke; howbeit yt is not of the best kynd, yt is but poore and weake, and of a byting tast."[64] Rolfe, however, had returned with seeds from Trinidad of *Nicotiana tabacum*. The first few barrels sent to London in 1614 were an immediate success.

Figure 123. *Taback de Nicotiaen*, engraving by Dutch physician and judge Johann van Beverwijck (1594 – 1647), from *Schat Der Gesontheydt*. Amsterdam: Ian Iacobsz Schipper, 1660 dbnl.org, pp. 143-144.

---

[64] Strachey, William. The Historie of Travaile into Virginia Britannia, ed. R. H. Major. London: Printed for the Hakylut Society, 1849 AO, p. 121.

CH. 13 THE TRANSITION TOWARD MODERNITY

The colonies of Virginia, the Carolinas and Maryland launched intensive production of the plant, though it was very expensive to cultivate. It rapidly exhausted fertile soil, required constant attention and left its cultivators hungry many times, without recourses to feed themselves or their domestic livestock. As is well known, the southern colonies can be distinguished from the northern (New England) by not being unanimously Puritan and by attracting in the beginning adventurers with a reputation somewhat burned in their places of origin. The economic importance of the cultivation of tobacco (combined with the ambiguous politics of the English crown) produced from 1620 to 1644 dozens of decrees from the colonial Assembly of Virginia on the *hierba nicotiana* among other important agricultural products.[65]

---

[65] "For hemp also, both English and Indian, and for English flax and aniseeds, we do require and enjoin all householders of this colony, that have any of these seeds, to make trial therof the next season. ... [A]ll tobacco and sassafras be brought by the planters to the cape merchant till such time as all the goods now or hertofore sent for the magazine be taken off their hands at the prices agreed on .... [T]hat the cape merchant do accept of the tobacco of all and every the planters here in Virginia, eithor for goods or upon bills of exchange at three shillings the pound the best and 18 shillings the second sort. ... 7. That no man dispose of any of his tobacco before the minister be satisfied .... 18. That every freeman shall fence in a quarter of an acre of ground before Whitsuntide next to make a garden for planting of vines, herbs, roots &c subpoena ten pounds of tobacco a man. ... 33. That for defraying of such publique debts our troubles have brought upon us. There shall be levied 10 pounds of tobacco upon every male head above sixteen years of adge now living" (Mcilwaine, H. R. and J. P. Kennedy, eds. Laws Enacted by the First General Assembly of Virginia, Journal of the House of Burgesses of Virginia, vol. I. Richmond, 1905, Aug 2-4, 1619, 5 Mar 1624, p. 330; Hening, William Waller. The Statutes at Large: Being a Collection of all the Laws of Virginia from the First Session of the Legislature in the year 1619, vol. I. NY: Printed for the Editor by R. S. W. & G. Bartow, 1823 oll.libertyfund.org, pp. 122-129).

As touched upon in the previous chapter, King James VI and I anathematized in 1604 the use of the drug with not a little sarcasm:

Omnipotent power of Tobacco! And if it could by the smoke therof chace our deuils, as the smoke of Tobias fish did (which I am sure could smel no stronglier) it would serue for a precious Relicke, both for the superstitious Priests, and the insolent Puritanes, to cast our deuils withall.[66]

The monarch combined his anathemas against smokers with a monopoly and a tax by weight on the cargo received in English ports, which soon became a formidable source of revenue. In 1628, the Governor and Councell replied to his monopoly

in a firm, but respectful manner, the injuries to which the planters in Virginia had been subjected by the mere report that their tobacco was to be monopolised in England; that it had so discouraaged the adventurers, that ... having no assurance of enjoying the fruits of their labour; and seeing that all contracts had heretofore been concluded in England without their consent. ... They then propose to contract with the king for all their tobacco, at *three shillings and six pence* per pound .... They request the king to take at least 500,000 weight, at the above price .... In the event of the king's acceding to their terms, they request the importation of Spanish tobacco may be prohibited.[67]

In Virginia the production of this plant was practically a monoculture, providing more than half the earnings from exports. William and Mary College, the second oldest American institution of learning was founded in 1693 through a royal charter which transferred the right of the king to collect a penny a pound on the tobacco exported from Virginia and Maryland

---

[66] James VI and I. A Covnter-Blaste to Tobacco, ed. Edmund Goldsmid. Edinburgh: Privately Printed, 1884 (London: R. B., 1604) AO, p. 25.
[67] Hening, 1823, 26 Mar 1628, pp. 134-135.

to make, found and establish a certain place of universal study ... [We] extend our royal bounty and munificence towards the erection and foundation of the said college ... in such case there should be paid to our said uncle [Charles II], and his heirs and successors, one penny for every pound of tobacco so loaded and put on board ... to apply and lay out the same, for building and adjoining the edifices and other necessities for the said college ....[68]

This was increased decades later by participation in a tariff on liquors imported from Europe.

In other countries, especially in those non-exporting, the reaction to the new drug achieved extremes of great virulence. In the middle of the seventeenth century, Czar Michael Fedorovitch Romanov (Michael I, 1596 – 1645) decreed a strict prohibition of tobacco on pain of the death penalty, torture, confiscation of property, beating with the knout, slitting of the nostrils and cutting off of the nose. A traveler witnessed the effects of one of its horrific punishments almost as soon as it was enacted:

Tobacco was heretofore fo common there, that is was generally taken, both in fmoak and powder. To prevent the mifchiefs occafion'd by the ufe of it, which were not onely, that the poorer fort of people ruin'd themfelves thereby, in as much as if they had but a peny, they would rather beftow it in Tobacco than bread, but alfo becaufe many times it fet houfes on fire, and thofe that took it prefented themfelves with their ftinking and infectious breaths before their Images, the Great Duke and the Patriarch thought fit in the year 1634. abfolutely to forbid the fale and ufe of it. Thofe who are convicted of having either taken or fold any, are very rigoroufly punifh'd. They have their Noftrils flit, or are whipp'd, as we have often feen done .... Whipping, as it is given in *Mufcovy*, is one of the moft barbarous punifhments that ever were heard of. *Sept.* 24. 1634. I faw eight men and one woman Whipt, for felling Aquavitae and Tobacco. The Executioner ... lay'd on their backs with all his ftrength, fo as that the blood gufh'd out at every lafh. ... Being thus difciplin'd, fo as

[68] 8 Feb 1693, XV, swem.wm.edu.

that their backs werein a manner flic'd and flafh'd all over, yet were they tied by the Arms, two and two together; thofe who had fold Tobacco having a little horn of it, and thofe who had fold Aquavitae, a little bottle about their Necks, and whipt through the Citie .... This is fo cruel a punifhment; that fome die of it ....[69]

His successor, Czar Alexsei Michailovitch (1629 – 1676) repeated this anti-tobacco legislation in the first written compendium of Russian laws, the law code (*ulozhenie*) of 1649:

11. In the past year 1633/1634 by the decree of the great Sovereign, Tsar, and Grand Prince of all Russia Mikhail Fedorovitch of blessed memory, a strict prohibition on tobacco was enacted in Moscow and in the provincial towns on pain of the death penalty, that Russians and various foreigners were not to keep tobacco in their possession anywhere, to sniff it, or to trade in tobacco. ... Now the Sovereign, Tsar, and Grand Prince of all Russia Aleksei Mikhailovitch has decreed ... 16. If musketeers, and wanderers, and various people are brought in for arraignment with tobacco twice, or thrice: torture those people many times, beat them with the knout on the rack, or around the market places. For [further] arraignments slit the nostrils and cut off the noses of such people.[70]

The renewal of the precepts indicates the phenomenon of illegalism or derogation by unfulfillment, but various public powers continued imposing the prohibition anyway.

Until the end of the century, in 1691, the German region of Luneberg surpassed this initiative and decreed the sentence of death for chewing, snuffing or inhaling tobacco smoke. On 30 January 1642

---

[69] Olearius, Adam. The Voyages & Travels of the Ambassadors from the Duke of Holstein, to the Great Duke of Muscovy, and the King of Persia, tr. John Davies. London: Printed for Thomas Dring and John Starkey, 1562 AO, The Third Book, The Second Voyage into Mufcovy and Perfia, June 1636, pp. 83, 123-124.

[70] The Law Code (Ulozhenie) of 1649, chapter 25, Statute on Illicit Taverns, In it are 21 articles, pages.uoregon.edu, based on Hellie, Richard, ed. The Muscovite Law Code (*Ulozhenie*) of 1649. NY: Charles Schlacks, 1988; Cfr. Szasz, 1985, pp. 185-186.

CH. 13 THE TRANSITION TOWARD MODERNITY

Pope Urban VIII issued a bull whose first words were *Cum Ecclesiae Divino*

directed against the wholesale consumption of tobacco in churches under the jurisdiction of Seville ... [because] "there was not a canon, chaplain or cleric, in fact no lay person of either sex who, either while they were performing their service in the choir and at the altar, or while they were listening to the Mass and the divine offices, were not at the same time, and with great irreverence, taking tobacco; and with fetid excrements sullying the altar, holy places and pavements of that diocese."[71]

The bull carried the punishment *ex communicationis latae fententiae* (sentence of excommunication) for an *abufus tam fcandalofus* (abuse so scandalous) on the grounds of the diocese, thinking of the clergy.[72] Eight years later any use of tobacco will be prohibited in Bavaria, Saxony and the canton of Zurich. In 1640 the last Ming emperor capitally punished the traffic and consumption, specifically with strangulation.[73] The then Shah of Persia also decreed the death penalty

---

[71] Tedeschi, John. "Literary Piracy in Seventeenth-Century Florence: Giovanni Battista Neri's *'De iudice S. inquisitionis opusculum,'*" *Huntington Library Quarterly*, vol. 50, no. 2 (Spring, 1987), University of Pennsylvania Press, pp. 109, 111, quoting Benedetto Stella, *Il Tabacco Opera*. Roma: Per Filippo Maria Mancini, 1669 AO, cap. XXXIII, *Se il Tabacco mafticato in foglia, ò attratto in fumo guafti il digiuno naturale*, pp. 347-348: *non v'era Canonico, Cappellano, ò Clerico ... di detta Diocefi.*

[72] Cocquelines, Caroli. *Bullarum Privilegiorum ac Diplomatum Romanorum Pontificum Amplissima Collectio*, Tomus Sextus, Pars Secunda. Romae: Typis, et sumptibus Hieronymi Mainardi, 1760 AO, DCXC111, *Prohibio ne in Eccelfiis Civitatis, & Dioecefis Hifpalen. fumatur Tabbaccum*, p. 312; Stella, 1669, pp. 349-352; see also *Memorias de la Academia de Ciencias de Barcelona*, vol. XXV, 4, p. 19.

[73] According to the Chinese historian Wang Adine [*La Chine et le problème de l'opium*. Paris: A. Perdone, 1933] in spite of numerous executions the measure not only failed but induced a liking for smoking opium, until then only ingested orally. Thinking the same are Varenne (1973, p. 93), Aparicio (1972, p. 174), and Lewin (1970, p. 61).

for this abuse. In Saxony, Transylvania, Berne and Saint Gall, in the Low Countries and in Sweden the custom was made illegal with varying degrees of severity. The Swedish King Gustav II Adolph [1594 – 1632], for example, is said to have declared that "there is nothing in the world so abominable as that smoke, with exception of the German language."[74] The custom appeared as a new shame, foreign and intolerable.

Indeed, the Leiden physician Jean Leander published his *Traité du Tabac, ou Panacée Universelle* in 1626 describes the use of the drug by the Indian priests he calls *Buhiles*, who *se ravir en extase* (ravish themselves into ecstasy) and *interrogeaient le diable* (interrogate the devil) when they want to foretell the future:

When they want to know the outcome of something, they perfume themselves with tobacco to ravish themselves into ecstasy, and when in this state question the devil as to the subject about which they want to know. The priest, having been questioned, burns dry tobacco leaves, and, with a hollow stalk or a pipe such as in common use among us, draws in the smoke and is transported to the point of losing all contact with his surroundings as if in ecstasy, letting himself fall to the ground, where he lies for the rest of the day or night, completely relaxed and motionless. Then he pretends that he has talked with the devil and gives oracles, thus doing wrong to these unfortuate Indians.[75]

Yet the English historian William Camden (1551 – 1623), who claimed to have recorded the first use of tobacco in England when Sir Francis Drake rescued the ill-fated survivors at Roanoake, disagreed that tobacco turned Englishmen into savages:

---

[74] Cfr. Lewin, 1970, pp. 311-312, 316.

[75] *Les prêtres indiens ... trompant ainsi ces malheureux Indiens* (Depierris, H. A. *Physiologie Sociale: Le Tabac*. Paris: E. Flammarion, 1898 gallica.bnf.fr, p. 53, quoting the translation by Barthélemy Vincent); Andrews, George and A. Vinkenoog. The Book of Grass: An Anthology on Indian Hemp. NY: Grove Press, 1967 AO, p. 29.

CH. 13 THE TRANSITION TOWARD MODERNITY

Thefe were the firft (that I know of) that brought at their returne into *England*, the *Indian* Plant called Tobacco, or *Nicotiana* .... And certes fince that time it is growne fo frequent in vfe, and of fuch price, that many, nay the moft part, with an infatiable defire doe take of it ... infomuch that Tobacco fhops are fet vp in greater number then either Alehoufes or Tauernes. And as one faid, but falfely, the bodies of fuch Englifhmen, as are fo much delighted with this plant, did feeme to degenerate into the nature of the Sauages, becaufe they were carried away with the felfe-fame thing, beleeuing to obtaine and conferue their health by the felfe-fame meanes, as the barbarians did.[76]

In spite of everything, before the seventeenth century ends the habit of smoking or chewing the plant had invaded all the continents except Antarctica. It arrived in frozen tundras and hot deserts, cities and countrysides. There is not in the annals of humanity a custom that disseminated so widely and quickly. The quantity of smokers over and over again recommended a system of taxing the product, initially put in place by Spain, and then Portugal (1644), Austria (1670) and France (1674). The situation began to calm down only at the beginning of the eighteenth century, when Peter the Great [Pyotr Alekseivich I, 1672 – 1725] renounced torture and mutilation. Peter set out for England but on 1 February 1697 but

just before leaving Russia for his famous journey abroad, he issued an order permitting the use and public sale of tobacco "since there are large amounts of it in many homes among all classes of people," and it was being smuggled in from all

---

[76] Camden, William.   Annales of the Time and Royall History of the Famous Empress Elizabeth Queene of England France and Ireland &c, tr. Abraham Darcie. London: Printed for Beniamin Fifher, 1625 AO, the Third Booke, 1585, p. 107; *Et hi reduces Indicam, illam plantam quam Tabacam vocant & Nicotiam ... Ut Anglorum corpora, (quod falfe ille dixit) ... Barbari delectentur, & fanari fe poffe-credant* (Camdeni, Guilielmi. *Annalium Rerum Anglicarum et Hibernicarum, regnante Elizabetha*, volumen Secundum. London: Thomas Hearne, 1717 AO, Pars Tertia, anno 1585, p. 449).

directions. His real reason was to make it possible to collect the customs dues which were lost as long as the trade was illegal.[77]

In 1698 before leaving England

he gave to Lord [Marquis de] Carmarthen, for a sum of 20,000£ (or 48,000 rubles), to be paid down, as monopoly of the sale of tobacco in Russia to the amount of 3000 barrels, or one and a half million pounds, for one year, having once before, while still in Russia, made a similar lease to Orlenko [Orlenok], for two years, for only 15,000 rubles.[78]

Upon signature of the contract with the English company *Farmer's General*, Peter received as prepayment of customs duties 12,000£, roughly 28,000 rubles.[79] Also the Pope reconsidered his attitude on excommunication. In 1725, Benedict XIII decided to accept *the dry drunk* – the name by which the habit was then known – to "avoid the faithful the scandalous spectacle of ecclesiastic dignitaries escaping to sanctuary to smoke in secret."[80]

Naturally, such a polemic did not go unnoticed by the *literati*. The French playwright, actor and poet Jean-Baptiste Poquelin (1622 – 1673, stage name, Molière) begins *Dom Juan* with an ironic celebration of the new vice, tobacco:

---

[77] Frederiksen, O. J. "Virginia Tobacco in Russia under Peter the Great," *The Slavonic and East European Review*, American Series, Vol. 2, no. 1 (Mar, 1943), Cambridge University Press, p. 41, citing M. M. Bogoslovski. Petr I (1941), II, p. 287.

[78] Palmer, William. The Patriarch and the Tsar, vol. 5. London: Trubner and Co., 1876 AO, p. 1007.

[79] Palmer, 1876, p. 44.

[80] Lewin, 1970, p. 312.

CH. 13 THE TRANSITION TOWARD MODERNITY

SGANAREL, with a Tobacco-box in his Hand.

Whatever *Aristotle* and the whole Body of *Philofophers* may fay, theres nothing comparable to Tobacco; 'tis the reigning Paffion of your better fort of People, and he who lives without Tobacco, deserves not to live; it not only exhilarates and purges human Brains; but it alfo trains the Mind to Virtue, and by this one learns to become well-bred.[81]

Tobacco also possessed illustrious and unironic supporters. One of the first was the unfortunate explorer and statesman Sir Walter Raleigh (1552 – 1618). Accompanying the first settlers to his Roanoke Island plantation was the astronomer and mathematician Thomas Hariot (1560 – 1621) who recorded approvingly the medicinal and somewhat skeptically the spiritual use of the drug by the natives:

There is an herbe which is fowed a part by it felfe & is called by the inhabitants *vppówoc* .... The Spaniards generally call it *Tobacco* .... [I]t purgeth fuperfluous fleame & other groffe humors, openeth all the pores & paffages of the body: by which meanes the vfe thereof, not only preferueth the body from obftructions; but alfo if any be, fo that they have not beene of too long continuance, in fhort time breakest them; wherby their bodies are naturally preferued in health, & know not many greeuous difeafes wherewithall wee in England are oftentimes afflicted. This *Vppówoc* is of fo precious eftimation amongeft thē, that they thinke their gods are marueloufly delighted therwith: Wherupon fometime they make hallowed fires & caft fome of the pouder therein for a facrifice: being in a ftorme vppon the waters, to pacifie their gods, they caft fome vp into the aire and into the water: for a weare for fifh being newly fet vp, they caft fome therein and into the aire: alfo after an efcape of danger, they caft fome into the aire likewife.[82]

---

[81] Molière, Jean-Baptiste Poquelin, aka. The Works of Molière: French and English, Volume the Fourth. London: Printed for D. Browne & A. Miller, 1755 AO, *Don John, or the The Feast of the Statue*, Act I, Scene I, p. 245; *SGANARRELLE tenant une tabatiére. Quoi que puiffe dire Ariftote ... apprend avec lui à devenir honnête homme* (Moliere, 1755, *Dom Juan, ou Le Festin de Pierre*, Acte I, Scene I, p. 244).

[82] Hariot, Thomas. A Briefe and True Report of the New Found Land of Virginia.

Figure 124. *Die Truckene Trunkenheit* (The Dry Drunkenness), engraving by German poet Jakob Balde (1604 - 1668), frontispiece to *Die Truckene Trunkenheit*. Nurnberg: Michael Endter, 1658 digital.slub-dresden.de, p. 7.

NY: Dodd, Mead & Company, 1903 (1588) AO, The fecond part of fuche commodities as Virginia is knowne to yeelde for victuall and fuftenance of man's life, fol. C3 and following, p. 46/80.

2.   The Luck of Coffee.   In Europe coffee is especially reproached in the Protestant part just like tobacco. It is as if the favorable acceptance of opium in this region should produce a correlative rejection of any other novelty. Already in 1611 some German landowners put in place the system of prohibiting its diffusion along with rewards to make effective said measure. A century later the norm continued in vigor. The Lord of Waldeck, for example, offered 10 talents to whoever should denounce the infraction of his precept and punished it with a public beating and confiscation of goods; the Bishop/Prince W. von Paderborn decreed that to drink coffee was a privilege of the nobility, the clergy and high officials, forbidden to common burghers and peasants, adding that any infractions would incur the punishment of flagellation.

In England Charles the Second issued on 29 December 1675 a Proclamation for the Suppression of Coffee Houses because they had become the

great resort of Idle and disaffected persons to them, have produced very evil and dangerous effects; ... for that in such houses ... divers false, malitious and scandalous reports are devised and spread abroad to the Defamation of his Majestie's Government and to the Disturbance of the Peace and Quiet of the Realm: his Majesty hath thought fit and necessary, that the said Coffee Houses be (for the future) Put down, and suppressed ....[83]

Ten days later, in the face of violent opposition and street demonstrations, he issued a new proclamation extending the date of closure which was then promptly forgotten about altogether.

Frederick the Great (Frederick II of Prussia, 1712 – 1786) became "annoyed when he saw how much money was paid to foreign

---

[83] Ukers, William H. All About Coffee. NY: The Tea and Coffee Trade Journal Company, 1922, pp. 72-73.

coffee merchants"[84] and on 13 September 1777 issued a manifesto condemning coffee and extolling the virtues of beer:

It is disgusting to notice the increase in the quantity of coffee used by my subjects and the amount of money that goes out of the country in consequence. Everybody is using coffee. If possible, this must be prevented. My people must drink beer. His Majesty was brought up on beer, and so were his ancestors, and his officers. Many battles have been fought and won by soldiers nourished on beer; and the King does not believe that coffee-drinking soldiers can be depended upon to endure hardship or to beat his enemies in case of the occurrence of another war.[85]

After this stern advice failed, he issued in 1781 the *Déclaration du Roi concernant la vente du café brûlé*, creating a crown monopoly on roasting coffee restricted to the elite, which quickly devolved into a

veritable persecution. Discharged wounded soldiers were mostly employed ... following the smell of roasting coffee whenever detected, in order to seek out those who might be found without roasting permits. ... These deputies made themselves so great a nuisance, and became so cordially disliked, that they were called "coffee-smellers" [*kaffee-schnufflers*] by the indignant people.[86]

In spite of everything, the bad feeling toward this drug (and tea) continued in the north of Europe until well into the nineteenth century. The German physician, the father of modern pathology (who opposed evolution and the germ theory of disease) Rudolf Ludwig Karl Virchow (1821 – 1902), for example, penned a treatise on food and beverages in which he compared the passion of tea and coffee drinkers to that of wine and liquor drinkers:

---

[84] Ukers, 1922, p. 46

[85] Ukers, 1922, p. 46.

[86] Ukers, 1922, pp. 46-47.

"The coffee sisters and tea brothers, whose guilds the priests of tolerance have so favored, are no less subject to a fervent passion than the drinkers of wine and spirits [tr. gwr]."[87]

Greater tolerance was observed in the south and east of Europe, but neither were there polemics lacking. The first *café* opened in London around 1650 and soon there appeared emulations in Paris. The new drug excited commentaries by the French aristocrat (whose letters show up in Proust's *À la recherche du temps perdu*)[88] Marie de Rabutin-Chantal, marquise de Sévigné (1626 – 1696) in letters to her daughter and her literary friends which track neatly the changing views on coffee in the seventeenth century.

At first she considered it a fad: "So you have left off your coffee; mademoiselle de Méri has likewise driven it from her house in disgrace. After such a reverse, who would ever depend upon fortune?"[89] Four years later she was completely unsure:

Du Chêne has still an aversion to coffee; the friar thinks there is no harm in it. ... The physician you esteem ... advises coffee. Ah! my child, what is left for me to say on this subject? or how can I determine whether I am right or wrong? We very often blame the most beneficial thing in the world, and make choice of what is the

---

[87] *Die Kaffeeschwestern und Theebrüder ... Leidenschaft, wie die Wein= und Schnapstrinker* (Virchow, Rudolf. *Ueber Nahrungs- und Genussmittel*. Berlin: C. G. Lüderitz'sche Verlagsbuchhandlung, 1868 AO, pp. 49-50); Lewin, Louis. Phantastica. NY: E. P. Dutton & Company, Inc., 1964 AO, p. 256; see also duetsche-digitale-bibliothek.de.

[88] *"Sévigné n'aurait pas mieux dit!"* ("Sévigné could not have said it better!"), in Proust, Marcel. *Du Coté de Chez Swann*. Paris: Gaston Gallimard, 1919, p. 24, e.g.

[89] Sévigné, Marie de Rabutin-Chantal, marquise de. Letters of Madame de Sévigné, vol. IV. London: Printed for J. Walker et al., 1811 AO, CCCCXIII, Paris, Sunday evening, May 10, 1676, p. 40; *Vous voilà donc revenue du café ... peut-on compter sur la fortune?* (Sévigné, Marie de Rabutin-Chantal, marquise de. *Lettres de Madame de Sévigné*, Tome III. Paris: Librarie de L. Hachette et Cie, 1863 AO, 535. – *De Madame de Sévigné a Madame de Grignan, A Paris, dimanche au soir, 10e mai* [1676], p. 313).

most pernicious, and, at best, grope in the dark. ... Caderousse is constantly praising coffee; it makes some people fat, others thin: what contrarieties! I do not see how it is possible to say any thing certain of what is attended with such opposite effects.[90]

Nine years later the reputation of coffee, for her, is in tatters. She recommends rice gruel and chicken broth instead, though she still keeps a little coffee around:

Coffee is quite in disgrace; the chevalier thinks it heats him, and puts his blood in a ferment; and I, you know, always follow the lead, have likewise rejected it; rice-gruel supplies its place, and I keep coffee for the winter. ... Coffee is in disgrace here, and consequently I take none: I thought, however, that it did me some good at Brevanes; but I have given it up, notwithstanding. ... [I]t must heat your blood, and we would confine you to chicken-broth.[91]

But within a few months she is enjoying *café au lait*:

We have good milk here, and good cows; we are much disposed to skim the cream off this good milk, and to mix it with coffee and sugar; this, my child, is a very good thing, and will be a great comfort to me during Lent. Du Bois approves it for the stomach and colds, and this, in a word, is the milk-coffee, or coffee-milk ....[92]

---

[90] Sévigné, Marie de Rabutin-Chantal, marquise de. Letters of Madame de Sévigné, vol. 5. London: Printed for J. Walker, et al., 1811 AO, DCII, 16 February 1680, p. 256; *Du Chesne hait toujours le café; le Frère n'en dit point de mal. ... d'une chose où il y a tant d'expériences contraires* (Sévigné, *Lettres*, Tome VI, 1862 AO, 782. – *De Madame de Sévigné a Madame de Grignan, A Paris, vendredi, 16e fevrier* [1680], pp. 265-266).

[91] Sévigné, Letters, 1811, vol. 7, DCCC, 1 November 1689 and DCCCXIII, 23 November 1689, pp. 171, 203.

[92] Sévigné, Letters, 1811, vol. 9, DCCCLXXI, 29 January 1690, p. 49; *Nous avons ici de bon lait et de bonnes vaches ... en un mot, ce lait cafeté ou ce café laite* (Sévigné, Marie de Rabutin-Chantal, marquise de. Recueil Des Lettres de Madame de Sévigné, Tome Huitième. A Avignon: Chez Fr. Chambeau, 1804 AO, DCCLXIV, A la Même, Aux Rochers, dimanche 29 Janvier 1690, p. 199).

As well there were numerous pontifications by the medical class. Willis prescribed it in remedies or in place of remedies, even sending his patients sometimes to the coffee seller instead of the apothecary: "But as to the Affects of the Brain or nervous Stock, I do frequently prefcribe this drink fooner than anything elfe for their cure, and therefore am wont to fend the fick to the Coffee houses fooner than to the Apothecaries fhops."[93] In 1697 it is recommended as a therapeutic vehicle in a professional dissertation, though in another year a conference member considered it proven that it shortened one's life. In 1716 its capacity to facilitate intellectual work was lauded, and in 1718 it provoked apoplexy, inflamed the liver, caused nephritic colitis and was discovered to be the cause of the gastric ruin of Colbert.[94]

The Italian philosopher and naturalist Francesco Redi (1626 – 1697), who helped demolish the theory of spontaneous generation, in a laudatory poem to Tuscan wine condemned drinkers of the new drugs, chocolate, tea and coffee:

Quackish resources are things for a dunce.
Cups of Chocolate,
Aye, or tea,
Are not medicines
Made for me.
I would sooner take to poison,
Then a single cup set eyes on
Of that bitter and guilty stuff ye
Talk of by the name of Coffee.

---

[93] Willis, 1679, Part I, *Of the Diftempers commonly called* Hypochondriack, *which is fhown to be, for the moft part Convulfive: briefly alfo of* Chalybeats *or* Steel-Medicines, ch. XI, p. 98, section V, ch. III, *Of too Great or Depraved* Diaphorefis *or Sweating, and its Remedy*, pp. 101, 109; section VII, ch. III, *The Kinds, Preparations, and Forms of Opiates*, p. 155.
[94] Lewin, 1970, pp. 265-266.

Let the Arabs and the Turks
Count it 'mongst their cruel works:
Foe of mankind, black and turbid,
Let the throats of slaves absorb it.[95]

But Bach wrote a cantata with an aria lauding the new drug:

Ah! How sweet coffee tastes,
more delicious than a thousand kisses,
milder than muscatel wine.
Coffee, I have to have coffee,
and, if someone wants to
pamper me, ah, then fill up my coffee again![96]

Add that from the end of the seventeenth century the *cafés* of London, Paris, Rome, Vienna and Madrid also sold the so-called *eau heroique* cold, a heavily caffeinated infusion containing five parts per hundred of liquid opium.[97]

Speaking of coffee houses generally and specifically of *Le Procope* in the 6th arrondisement (founded in 1686, located across the street from the *Comédie-Française* and today the oldest Parisian *café* in continuous operation), the French philosopher and man of letters Baron de La Brède et de Montesquieu (1689 – 1755) commented:

---

[95] Redi, Francesco. <u>Bacchus in Tuscany</u>, tr. Leigh Hunt. London: Printed for John and H. L. Hunt, 1825 AO, pp. 11-12; *Non fia già, che il Cioccolate/ V' adopraBi, ovvero il Tè ... Sì nero, e torbido/ Gli shiavi ingollino* (Redi, Francesco. <u>Bacco in Toscana</u>. Firenze: Per Piero Matini, 1685 AO, pp. 9-10).

[96] *Ei! wie schmeckt der Coffee susse ... so schenkt mir Coffee ein! (Schweight Stille, plaudert nicht* (Be Still, Stop Chattering), BWV 211, the Bach Coffee Cantata, emmanuelmusic.org)

[97] Cfr. Behr, 1981, p. 62.

Coffee is very much used in Paris; there are a great many public houses where it may be had. In some of these they meet to gossip, in others to play at chess. There is one where the coffee is prepared in such a way that it makes those who drink it witty: at least, there is not a single soul who on quitting the house does not believe himself four times wittier than when he entered it.[98]

3.   The Points of Contact.   Like tobacco, coffee unconditionally won its battle toward the end of the eighteenth century. Soon the great coffee plantations spread from Ceylon and Indonesia to South America. Though its most active components were not yet known with precision, coffee became socially acceptable and many doctors considered the drug only lightly toxic in moderate doses.[99] Something similar was affirmed for tobacco, although its toxicity is incomparably greater.[100] Today the top four producers of tobacco are overwhelmingly China [2.8 million tons], followed by India, Brazil and the United States. Cuba is far down the list.[101]

---

[98] Montesquieu, Baron de La Brède et de. Persian Letters, vol. I, tr. John Davidson. London: Privately Printed, 1892 AO, Letter XXXVI, Usbek to Rhedi, at Venice, pp. 82-83.

[99] A cup of coffee has between 74-195 milligrams of caffeine [Death Wish Coffee is said to have 708], and one of tea between 16-70 mgs. Excessive use of coffee produces gastric illnesses, diarrhoea, headaches, insomnia, excitation, depression with muscular shaking, double vision, dizziness, ringing in the ears, loss of coordination, testicle pain, psychosis with delirium, vertigo, hypertension, brachycardia, paroxysmal atrial fibrilation, and in severe overdoses, tremor, convulsions, coma and death (cfr. Lewin, 1970, pp. 269-270; Inchem.org). Professional tea tasters suffer in the most grave cases stomach problems, headaches, hypochondria, loss of memory, vision defects and eventually atrophic cirrosis (cfr. Lewin, 1970, p. 275).

[100] Nicotine, used widely as an insecticide, is classified among the supertoxic (like cyanide and strichnine). Between 0.5 and 1.0 mg/kg is sufficient to kill an adult that has not developed a tolerance. A packet of cigarettes contains approximately 22 to 36 mg though a smoker only inhales 1.1 to 1.8 mg.

[101] The consumption of the latter touched a temporary ceiling around 2018, with

One could say that these new drugs have in common their being stimulants. What tobacco and coffee also have in common is *addictivity*. This can be measured by the percentage of occasional use that becomes compulsive use, and by falls from grace after the first attempt at abstinence, a phenomenon not unknown from the start.

In 1698 the Mexican Catholic historian and Franciscan brother Augustín de Vetancurt (1620 – 1700) listed tobacco's virtues:

which the Mexicans call Pizietl is hot and dry in the third degree, that using it as a medicine takes advantage of its virtues .... Smoking it makes one spit, cooks the phlegm, helps with asthma, amends the breath, comforts the head, provokes sleep, calms the stomach, heals women during their periods, takes away their fainting, and seems to drive away even death. Eating it relieves tooth and stomach pain, and makes men agile and prompt for any physical exercise.[102]

However, he added "that it is harmful if continued as a vice, which is well understood by the entire world."[103]

Agricultural peoples of the Amazon and Orinoco Basins, who chew tobacco but also consume very active visionary drugs (*yagé*, *ebene*), understand completely the difference between the former and the latter:

---

production worldwide (largely Chinese) nearing five thousand and three hundred cigarettes per smoker per year (World Health Organization, Internationally Peer Reviewed Chemical Safety Information, Inchem.org).

[102] *El Tabaco, que los Mexicanos llaman Pizietl ... promptos para qualquier exerficio corporal* (Vetancurt, Augustín de. *Teatro Mexicano*, Tom. I. En Mexico: por Doña Maria de Benavides Viuda de Iuan de Ribera, 1698 AO, *Tratado Segundo, De la fertilidad, y riqueza en comun de efte Nuevo Mundo, Cap. XI, De los arboles, y plantas medicinales, fus virtudes, y efectos*, p. 64).

[103] Vetancurt, 1698, p. 64.

Figure 125. Frontispiece, from Philippe Sylvestre Dufour's _Traités Novvevx & Cvrievx Dv Café Dv Thé et Dv Chocolate_. Lyon: Chez Iean Gerin, & B. Riiere, 1685.

Finally, it is worth noting that none of the hallucinogens used by Yanomanö are habit-forming .... Yanomanö can and do abstain from them for weeks and do not mention it or complain about it. Tobacco-chewing, on the other hand, is habitual: they cannot go several hours without it, and the entire village is in a state of crisis when the tobacco crop fails. When we are out of tobacco we crave it intensely and we say we are *hõri* – in utter poverty. We do not crave *ebene* in the same way and therefore never say we are 'in poverty' when there is none.[104]

In effect, to date there is not known a drug that, as Molière said, concentrates in a similar fashion *la paſſion des honrêtes gens* (the passion of your better sort of people). It is not accidental that the modern usage of the term *addiction* (referring to the compulsion and need to continue taking a drug) first appears in a text of 1779[105] by Samuel Johnson (1709 – 1784) and refers specifically to tobacco. It's also evident that tobacco's abstinence syndrome occurs much sooner than in the case of the most active opiates.

The same abstinence syndrome happens with coffee and its analogues (tea, *maté*, gurana, cola, chocolate, etc). In the 1940s it was scientifically known that 80 milligrams of caffeine [1,3,7 – Trimethyl xanthine] daily (equivalent to five cups of espresso or ten ground), absorbed during a week, is enough to produce such an effect. These timely experiments, which administered this dose over a week,

---

[104] Chagnon, Napoleon A, et al. "Yanomano Hallucinogens: Anthropological, Botanical, and Chemical Findings," *Current Anthropology*, vol. 12, no. 1, Feb. 1971, jstor.org, p. 74.

[105] "His addiction to tobacco is mentioned by one of his biographers, who remarks that in all his writings, except *Blenheim*, he has found an opportunity of celebrating the fragrant fume" (Johnson, Samuel. Lives of the English Poets, vol. I. London: Oxford University Press, 1799 AO, John Philips, p. 222); see also Ott, 1985, p. 7. "*Addictio* ... was ... the judicial act by which a debtor was made the slave of his creditor" (Rosenthal, R. J. and Faris, Suzanne. "The etymology and early history of 'addiction,'" *Addiction Research and Theory*, 27 (2), February 2019 researchgate.net, p. 3).

followed by a placebo, created in eighty-four percent of the subjects a neat clinical picture. Fifty-five percent, a few hours after receiving the placebo were overcome by the worst headache of their lives, accompanied by nausea, vomiting, muscular tension, anxiety, inability to work and lethargy.[106] Twenty-nine percent of the rest suffered an analogous reaction but weaker. This data was checked two decades later by another group of investigators.[107] Similar experiments with chocolate show a basically identical syndrome. With 600 milligrams daily of theobromine (dimethyl xanthine) continued for a week, one can produce practically the same syndrome in cases of abstention.[108]

This does not help to explain a diatribe launched by one Johannes Franciscus Rauch in Vienna in 1624 where he maintained that chocolate inflamed the passions and and ought to be prohibited categorically to the clergy:

The immoderate use of chocolate in the seventeenth century was considered as so violent an inflamers of the passions, that Joan. Franc. Rauch published a treatise against it, and enforced the necessity of forbidding the *monks* to drink it; and adds, that if such an interdiction had existed, that scandal with which that holy order had been branded might have proved more groundless.[109]

His fellow monks were not amused and the work, the

---

[106] See, for example, Dreisbach, R. H. et al. "Caffeine withdrawl headache," *Journal of Laboratory and Clinical Medicine*, 28, 1212, 1943.

[107] Goldstein, A. et al. "Psychotropic effects of caffeine in man," *Clin. Pharm. and Therapeutics*, 10, 1969, pp. 477 and 489.

[108] Ott, J. The Cacahuatl Eater. Vashon, WA: 1985, p. 80.

[109] Disraeli, Isaac. Curiosities of Literature, vol. II, ed. Benjamin Disraeli. London: Routledge, Warne, and Routledge, 1863 AO, Introduction of Tea, Coffee, and Chocolate, p. 325; Ott, 1985, p. 91.

Disputatio medico-diaetetica de aëre et esculentis, necnon de potú, Vienna, 1924, is a *rara avis* among collectors. This attack on the monks, as well as on chocolate, is said to be the cause of its scarcity; for we are told that they were so dilligent in suppressing this treatise, that it is supposed not a dozen copies exist.[110]

But its virtues as a soft cardiac tonic, which it shares with other stimulants, explains the custom of making bonbons and boxes of bonbons in the shape of hearts. Lovers are giving something that does not merit being called an inflamer of passions, though it does help to keep them awake.

---

[110] Disraeli, 1863, p. 325.

Bibliography
Volume Two Part Two

Acosta, Cristóbal. *Tractado de las Drogas, y medicinas de la Indias Orientales*. Burgos: Por Martin de Victoria, 1578

Agrippa, Henry Cornelius. The Vanity of Arts and Sciences. London: Samuel Speed, 1676

Agrippae ab Nettesheym, Henrici Cornelii. De incertitudine & vanitate omnium fcientiarum & artium. Lvgdvni: *Excudebat Severinvs Matthaei*, 1643

Alpini, Prospero. *Histoire naturelle de l'Egypte*, tr. R. de Fenoyl. Caire: Institut français d'archéologie orientale du Caire, 1979

Amador de los Rios, José. *Historia Social, Política y Religiosa de los Judíos de España y Portugal*, vol. III. Madrid: T. Fortanet, 1876

Andragoya, Pascual de. Narrative of the Proceeding of Pedrarius Davila, tr. Clements R. Markham. London: Printed for the Hakluyt Society, 1865

Andrews, George and A. Vinkenoog. The Book of Grass: An Anthology on Indian Hemp. NY: Grove Press, 1967

Aparicio, O. *Drogas y toxicomanías*. Madrid: Editora Nacional, 1972

Ayrault, P. *Ordre et Instruction Judiciare*, book III. Paris: *A. Cotillon et Cie/A. Chevalier-Marescq*, 1881

------------- *De L'ordre et Instruction Judiciare*. Paris: *Chez Jacques du Puys*, 1576

Balde, Jakob. *Die Truckene Trunkenheit*. Nurnberg: Michael Endter, 1658

Barbosa, Duarte. Description of the Coasts of East Africa and Malabar in the beginning of the sixteenth century, tr. Henry E. J. Stanley. London: Printed for the Hakylut Society, 1866

Barbosa, Duarte. *Livro Em que dá relação do que viu e ouviu no Oriente*. Lisboa: *Divisão de Publicações e Biblioteca, Agência Geral das Colónias*, 1946

Barrett, W. P., tr. The Trial of Jeanne D'Arc. NY: Gotham House, Inc., 1932

Battum, Carolum. *Secreet-Boeck Van veel diverfche en Heerlijcke Konften in veelderleye Materien*. Amsterdam: Jan Wilting, 1656

Behr, Hans-Georg. *La droga, potencia mundial.* Barcelona: 1981 (*Weltmacht Droge, Das Geschaft mit der Sucht*. Wien/Dusseldorf: 1980)

Blázquez Miguel, Juan. *La Inquisición en Castilla-La Mancha*. Madrid: Pub. Univ. de Córdoba, 1986

Bodin, Jean. *De la Demonomanie des Sorciers*. Paris: *Chez Iacqves Dv-Pvys*, 1587

Boë, Frans de le. Of Childrens Diseases, given in a familiar style for weaker capacities, tr. Richard Gower. London: George Downs, 1682

Boquet, Henry. *Discovrs Execrable des Sorciers*. Paris: Chez Denis Binet, 1603

Bori, Pier Cesare (1937 – 2012), tr. The Pico Project/*Progetto Pico*, a collaboration between Brown and the University of Bologna

Boyd, Eldon M. and Marion L. MacLachlan. "The Expectorant Action of Paregoric," *Canadian Medical Association Journal*, vol. 50, no. 4, April 1944

Boyle, Robert. Some Considerations touching the Vsefvlnesse of Experimental Naturall Philofophy. Oxford: Printed by Hen: Hall, 1663

Brau, Jean-Louis. *Historia de la droga* (orig. *Histoire de la drogue*). Barcelona: Bruguera, 1973

Brecher, E. M. Licit and Illicit Drugs. Boston: Little Brown, 1972

BIBLIOGRAPHY

Brunschwygk [Brunschwig], Hieronymus. *Liber de arte Diftillandi de Compofitis*. Straussberg: Johann Gruninger, 1512

Buckland, W. W. ed. The Digest of Justinian, tr. C. H. Munro, vol. I, 2. 1. 3. Cambridge, UK: at the University Press, 1904

Buckley, Theodore Alois, tr. Canons and Decrees of the Council of Trent. London: George Routledge and Co., 1851

Burkhardt, Carl Jacob Christoph. The Civilization of the Renaissance in Italy: 1860 – 1878, tr. S. G. C. Middlemore. NY: Modern Library, 2002

Calderón de la Barca, Pedro. *La Vida es Sueno*. Madrid: Librerias de la Viuda É Hijos de Cuesta, 1881

California Department of Public Health Factsheet March 2018, cdph.ca.gov

Camden, William. Annales of the Time and Royall History of the Famous Empress Elizabeth Queene of England France and Ireland &c, tr. Abraham Darcie. London: Printed for Beiamin Fifher, 1625

Camdeni, Guilielmi. *Annalium Rerum Anglicarum et Hibernicarum, regnante Elizabetha*, volumen Secundum. London: Thomas Hearne, 1717

Caponigri, Robert A., tr. Oration on the Dignity of Man. Chicago, IL: Regnery Gateway, 1956

Cárdenas, Iuan de. *Primera Parte de los Problemas y Secretos Marauillosos de las Indias*. En Mexico: Casa de Pedro Ocharte, 1591

Carlos II. *Recopilacion de Leyes de los Reynos de las Indias*, vol. II. Madrid: Por la viuda de D. Joaquin Ibarra, 1791

Caro Baroja, Julio. *Las brujas y su mundo*. Madrid: Alianza Editorial, 1966

----------------------- *El Señor Inquisidor y otras vidas por oficio*. Madrid: Alianza Editorial, 1968

----------------------- *Inquisición, brujería y criptojudaismo*. Barcelona: Ariel, 1970

----------------------- The World of the Witches, O. N. V. Glendinning, tr. Chicago: University of Chicago Press, 1971

----------------------- The World of the Witches, Glendinning, Nigel, tr. London: Phoenix Press, 2001

Casas, Fray Bartolomé de las. *Historia de las Indias*, ed. Augustín Millares Carlo, vol. I. Mexico, DF: Fondo de Cultura Economica, 1951

Chagnon, Napoleon A, et al. "Yanomano Hallucinogens: Anthropological, Botanical, and Chemical Findings," *Current Anthropology*, vol. 12, no. 1, Feb. 1971

Chisholm, Hugh, ed. The Encyclopaedia Britannica, vol. VII, Constantine Pavlovich to Demidov. Cambridge, UK: at the University Press, 1910

----------------------- The Encyclopaedia Britannica, vol. XIII, Harmony to Hurstmonceaux. Cambridge, England: at the University Press, 1910

----------------------- The Encyclopaedia Britannica, vol. XVI, L to Lord Advocate. Cambridge, UK: at the University Press, 1911

----------------------- The Encyclopaedia Britannica, vol. XXIII. NY: The Encyclopaedia Britannica Company, 1911

----------------------- The Encyclopaedia Britannica, vol. XXVII. Cambridge, UK: at the University Press, 1911

Clark, A. J. "Appendix V – Flying Ointments" found in Murray, Margaret Alice. The Witch-Cult in Western Europe. Oxford: at the Clarendon Press, 1921

Cocquelines, Caroli. *Bullarum Privilegiorum ac Diplomatum Romanorum Pontificum Amplissima Collectio, Tomus Sextus, Pars Secunda. Romae: Typis, et sumptibus Hieronymi Mainardi*, 1760

BIBLIOGRAPHY

Coresão, Armando, tr. <u>The Suma Oriental of Tomé Pires</u>, vol. II. London: Printed for the Hakylut Society, 1944

Correvon, Gabriel Seigneux de. *Observations sur des matières de jurisprudence criminelle*, tr. Paul Risi. Lausanne, CH: *Chez Franç Grasset et Comp.*, 1768

Cortés, Hernán. *Cartas de Relación de la Conquista de Méjico*, vol. I. Madrid: Calpe, 1922

Cosenza, Mario Emilio. <u>Biographical and Bibliographical Dictionary of the Italian Humanists 1300 – 1800</u>, vol. 5, second edition. Boston: G. K. Hall, 1962-1967

D la Vega, Garcilaso. *Los Comentarios Reales D Los Incas*, vol. II, ed. Horacio H. Urteaga. Lima: Imp. y Libreria Sanmarti y Ca., 1919

Davidson, J., tr. <u>Montesquieu: Persian Letters</u>, London: George Routledge & Sons LTD, 1891

Dalton, J. C. <u>Galen and Paracelsus</u>. NY: D. Appleton and Company, 1873

De Acosta, Padre Iofeph. *Historia Natvral y Moral de las Indias*. Madrid: en cafa de Alonfo Martin, 1608

Delacoste, J., ed. <u>Boerhaave's Aphorisms: Concerning the Knowledge and Cure of Diseases</u>. London: Printed for B. Cowfe, and W. Innys, 1715

De Lancre, Pierre. *Tableuv de L'inconstance des Mavvais Anges et Demons*. Paris: Chez Iean Berjon, 1612

De la Vega, Garcilasso. <u>First Part of the Royal Commentaries of the Yncas</u>, vol. II, tr. Clements R. Markham. London: Printed for the Hakluyt Society, 1871

Deleboe, Francisci, Sylvii. *Opera Medica*. Amstelodami: Apud Danielem Elsevirium et Abrahamum Wolfgang, 1679

De León, Pedro de Cieza. *La Crónica del Perú*, part one. Madrid: Calpe, 1922

Depierris, H. A. *Physiologie Sociale: Le Tabac.* Paris: E. Flammarion, 1898

Diaz del Castillo, Capitan Bernal. *Historia Verdadera de la Conquista de la Nueva España*, vol. II. Paris: Libreria de Rosa, 1837

Disraeli, Isaac. Curiosities of Literature, vol. II, ed. Benjamin Disraeli. London: Routledge, Warne, and Routledge, 1863

Douglas, M. Natural Symbols: Explorations in Cosmology. NY: Pantheon Books, 1970

Dover, Thomas. The Ancient Physician's Legacy to his Country. London: Printed for the Author, 1732

Dreisbach, R. H. et al. "Caffeine withdrawl headache," *Journal of Laboratory and Clinical Medicine*, 28, 1212, 1943

Dufour, Philippe Sylvestre. *Traités Novvevx & Cvrievx Dv Café Dv Thé et Dv Chocolate.* Lyon: Chez Iean Gerin, & B. Riiere, 1685.

Escalona, Gaspare de. *Gazophilacium Regium Perubicum.* Matriti: Ex Typographia Blasii Roman, 1775

Estopañan, Cirac. *Los procesos de hechicería en la Inquisición de Castilla la Nueva.* Madrid: *Instituto Jerónimo Zurita* (CSIC), 1942

Feyjoó y Montenegro, Benito Geronymo. *Cartas eruditas y curiosas*, vol. 4. Madrid: *Por D. Joachin Ibarra*, 1770

Firth, C. W. and R. S. Rait, eds. Acts and Ordinances of the Interregnum 1642 – 1660, vol. II. London: Published by His Majesty's Stationery Office, 1911

Folsom, George, tr. The Despatches of Hernando Cortes. NY: Wiley and Putnam, 1843

Font Quer, P. *Plantas Medicinales, El Dioscorides renovado.* Barcelona: Labor, 1982

BIBLIOGRAPHY

Foucault, Michel. Discipline and Punish, tr. Alan Sheridan. New York: Vintage Books, 1995

Frederiksen, O. J. "Virginia Tobacco in Russia under Peter the Great," *The Slavonic and East European Review*, Ameican Series, Vol. 2, no. 1 (Mar, 1943), Cambridge University Press

Gagliano, Joseph A. "The Coca Debate in Colonial Peru," *The Americas*, vol. 20, no. 1 (Jul 1963), Cambridge University Press, jstor.org

Garza, Mercedes de la. *Sueno y alucinacion en el mundo nahuatl y maya*. Mexico, DF: Instituto de Investigaciones Filogicas, UNAM, 1990

Gifford, George. A Dialogue Concerning Witches & Witchcrafts. London: Printed for the Percy Society, 1842

Goade, Richard, tr., ed. Herman Boerhaave's Materia Medica, or the Druggists' Guide. London: Printed for the Author, 1755

Goldstein, A. et al. "Psychotropic effects of caffeine in man," *Clin. Pharm. and Therapeutics*, 10, 1969

Grinspoon, L. and J. Bakalaar. *La cocaína: una droga y su evolución social*. Barcelona: Hacer, 1982

Hariot, Thomas. A Briefe and True Report of the New Found Land of Virginia. NY: Dodd, Mead & Company, 1903 (1588)

Harper, R. F., tr. The Code of Hammurabi. Chicago, IL: University of Chicago Press, 1904

Harris, Marvin. Cows, Pigs, Wars, and Witches: The Riddles of Culture. NY: Vintage Books, 1974

Harsnett, Samuel. A Declaration of Egregious Popifh Impoftures. London: Printed by James Roberts, 1603

865

Hartman, John, tr. Bazilica Chymica, & Praxis Chymiatricae OR Royal and Practical Chymistry. London: John Starkey et al 1670

Hartmann, Franz. The Life and the Doctrines of Paracelsus. NY: Macoy Publishing and Masonic Supply Company, 1945

Hegel, George Wilhelm Frederich. Encyklopädie der Philosophischen Wissenschaften. Leipzig: Verlag der Bürrschen Buchhandlung, 1870

--- On Christianity: Early Theological Writings, Knox, T. M. and Richard Kroner, trs. NY: Harper & Brothers, 1948

Helmont, John Baftifa Van. Oriatrike, or Phyfick Refined, tr. John Chandler. London: Printed for Lodowick Loyd, 1662

Hening, William Waller. The Statutes at Large: Being a Collection of all the Laws of Virginia from the First Session of the Legislature in the year 1619, vol. I. NY: Printed for the Editor by R. S. W. & G. Bartow, 1823

Hernández de Toledo, Francisco. Rervm Medicarvm Novae Hispaniae Thesavrus, ed. A Nardo Antonio Reechi. Romae: Vitalis Mascardi, 1651

Hodge, Frederick Webb, ed. Handbook of American Indians North of Mexico, part 2. Washington, DC: Government Printing Office, 1910

Holmes, Edward Morel. "Pharmacopoeia," The Encyclopaedia Britannica, vol. 21, eleventh edition. Cambridge, UK: at the University Press, 1911

Hull, Gillian. "The Influence of Herman Boerhaave," Journal of the Royal Society of Medicine, vol. 90, September 1997

Jarman, B. G. and R. Russell, chief eds. The Oxford Spanish Dictionary, fourth ed. Oxford, UK: Oxford University Press, 2008

James VI and I. <u>Daemonologie</u>. Edinburgh: Printed by Arnold Hatfield for Robert Wald-graue, 1597

---------------------- <u>A Covnter-Blaste to Tobacco</u>, ed. Edmund Goldsmid. Edinburgh: Privately Printed, 1884 (1604)

---------------------- <u>A Royal Rhetorician</u>, ed. Robert S. Rait. Westminster: A Constable and Co., 1900

Johnson, Samuel. <u>Lives of the English Poets</u>, vol. I. London: Oxford University Press, 1799

Kelekna, Pita. "Farming, Feuding, and Female Status: the Achuar Case," in <u>Amazonian Indians from Prehistory to Present: Anthropological Perspectives</u>, ed. Anna Roosevelt. Tucson, AZ: University of Arizona Press, 1994

Klerk, Saskia. "The Trouble with Opium," *Early Science and Medicine* 19 (2014), Brill, academia.edu

Kuo, P. C. <u>A Critical Study of the First Anglo-Chinese War with Documents</u>. Taipei: Ch'eng Wen Publishing Co., 1970 (1935)

Laguna, Andrés de, tr. *Pedacio Dioscorides Anazarbeo, acerca de la materia medicinal, y de los venenos mortiferos*. Salamanca: *Por* Mathias Gast, 1563

Lamas, Andrés. *Introduccion*, in Lozano, Pedro. *Historia de la Conquista del Paraguay*, vol. I, ed. Andrés Lamas. Buenos Aires: Casa Editora Imprenta Popular, 1873

Larousse, Pierre. *Grand Dictionnaire Universel du XIXe Siècle*, vol. 14. Paris: Administration de Grand Dictionnaire Universel, 1875

Laurière, Eusèbe de. *Ordonnance des Roys de France de la troisieme race*, vol. 2. Paris: De L'Imprimerie Royale, 1729

Lea, Henry Charles. <u>A History of the Inquisition in Spain</u>, vol. I. NY: Macmillan Company, 1908

------------------------ A History of the Inquisition of the Middle Ages, vol. III. NY: The MacMillan Company, 1922

Leopold, J. H., ed. *M. Antoninus Imperator Ad Se Ipsum*, IX, 2. Leipzig: B. G. Teubneri, 1908

Levillier, Roberto, ed. *Gobernantes del Peru*, Cartas y Papeles, Siglo XVI, vol. VIII. Madrid: Imprenta de Juan Pueyo, 1925

Lévi-Strauss, Claude. Structural Anthropology, trs. Claire Jacobson and Brooke Grundfest Schoepf. NY: Basic Books, 1963

Lewin, Louis. Phantastica. NY: E. P. Dutton & Company, Inc., 1964

-------------------------------- Paris: Payot, 1970

Long, George, tr. The Thoughts of the Emperor M. Aurelius Antoninus. Boston: Tichnor and Fields, 1864

------------------------ The Thoughts of Marcus Aurelius Antoninus, with an essay by Matthew Arnold. London: G. Bell and Sons, Ltd., 1913

Lozano, Pedro. *Historia de la Conquista del Paraguay*, vol. I, ed. Andres Lamas. Buenos Aires: Casa Editora Imprenta Popular, 1873

Major, R. H., tr., ed. Select Letters of Christopher Columbus. London: Printed for the Hakluyt Society, 1870

Malebranche, Nicolas. *De la Recherche de la Vérité, Oeuvres de Malebranche*, vol. III, ed. J. Simon. Paris: Charpentier, 1871

Mans, Pierre Belon du. *Les Observations de Plvsievrs Singvlaritez et Choses Memorables*. Paris: *Chez Hierofme de Marnef*, 1588

Marwick, Max, ed. Witchcraft and Sorcery. UK: Penguin Books, 1970

Matienzo, Juan. *Gobierno del Perú*. Buenos Aires: Compañía Sud-Americana de Billetes de Banco, 1910

Matthioli, Petri Andreae. *Commentarij in VI. libros Pedacij Diofcoridis Anazarbei de Medica materia*. *Venetijs: Felicem Valgrifium*, 1583

BIBLIOGRAPHY

Mcilwaine, H. R. and J. P. Kennedy, eds. Laws Enacted by the First General Assembly of Virginia, Journal of the House of Burgesses of Virginia, vol. I. Richmond, 1905

Midelfort, H. C. Erik. Witch Hunting in Southwestern Germany 1562 – 1684. Stanford, CA: Stanford University Press, 1972

Molière, Jean-Baptiste Poquelin, aka. The Works of Molière: French and English, Volume the Fourth. London: Printed for D. Browne & A. Miller, 1755

Molina, Alonfo de. *Vocabvlario en lenqva castellana y mexicana.* En Mexico: En Cafa de Antonio de Spinofa, 1571

Monardes, Nicolas. *Primera y Segvnda y Tercera Partes de La Historia Medicinal.* Sevilla: En cafa de Alonfo Efcriuano, 1574

------------------------ Joyfull Newes Out of the New-found Worlde, English'd by John Frampton. London: Printed by E. Allde, by the afsigne of Bonhams Norton, 1596

Montaigne, Michel Eyquem de. Essays of Montaigne, tr. Charles Cotton, vol. III. London: Reeves and Turner, 1877

-- *Les Essais de Michel, Seignevr de Montaigne.* Paris: Chez Charles Angot, 1657

Montesquieu, Charles-Louis de Secondat, Baron de la Brède et de. *Lettres Persanes,* ed. R. Loyalty. NY: Oxford University Press, 1914

Motolinia, Toribio de Benavente o. *Historia de los Indios de la Nueva España.* Barcelona: Herederos de Juan Gili, Editores, 1914

Navarette, Martin Fernández de. *Coleccion de los viajes y descubrimiento,* vol. III. Madrid: En la Imprenta Real, 1829

Nohl, Herman, ed. *Hegel's Theologifche Jugendfchriften.* Tubingen: Berlag von J. C. B. Mohr (Paul Siebeck), 1907

Olearius, Adam. The Voyages & Travels of the Ambassadors from the Duke of Holstein, to the Great Duke of Muscovy, and the King of Persia, tr. John Davies. London: Printed for Thomas Dring and John Starkey, 1562

Orta, Garcia da. Colloquies on the Simples & Drugs of India, tr. Sir Clements Markham, ed. Conde de Ficalho. London: Henry Sotheran and Co., 1913

-------------------- *Coloquios dos Simples E Drogas Da India*, ed. Conde de Ficalho, vol. II. Lisboa: *Imprensa Nacional*, 1892

Ott, J. The Cacahuatl Eater. Vashon, WA: 1985

Oviedo y Valdés, Gonzalo Fernandez de. *Historia general y natural de las indias*, primera parte, ed. José Amador de los Rios. Madrid: Imprenta de la Real Academia de la Historia, 1851

Palmer, William. The Patriarch and the Tsar, vol. 5. London: Trubner and Co., 1876

Pané, Ramón. *Relación Acerca de las Antigüedades de los Indios*, ed. Josē Juan Arrom. Madrid: Siglo Veintiuno, 1968

Paracelsi Bombast ab Hohenheim, Avr. Philip. Theoph. *Opera Omnia*, vol. I. Geneva: Sumptibus Ioan. Antonij, & Samuelis De Tournes, 1658

Pardo-Tomás, José. "Natural knowledge and medical remedies in the book of secrets: uses and appropriations in Juan de Cárdenas' *Problemas y secretos maravillosos de las Indias* (Mexico, 1591)," [Barcelona: CSIC] in Passion for Plants: Materia Medica and Botany in Scientific Networks from the 16th to 18th centuries, ed. Sabine Anagnostou et al. Stuttgart: Wissanschafliche Verlagsgesellshaft mbH, 2011

Parent, André. "Franciscus Sylvius on Clinical Teaching, Iatrochemistry and Brain Anatomy," *The Cambridge Journal of Neurological Sciences*, 2016

Partington, J. R. "Joan Baptista van Helmont," *Annals of Science*, vol. I, no. 4, 15 Oct 1936

Pemberton, H., tr. The Dispensatory of the Royal College of Phyficians, London. London: Printed for T. Longman and T. Shewell ... and J. Nourse, 1746

Perez de Barradas, J. *Plantas Magicas Americanas*. Madrid: CSIC, 1957

Poma de Ayala, Felipe Guaman. *Nueva Corónica y Buen Gobierno*. Caracas: Biblioteca Ayacucho, 1980

-- The First New Chronicle and Good Government, tr., ed. Roland Hamilton. Austin: University of Texas Press, 2009 (1615)

Pomponatii Mantva, Pietri. *De Naturalium effectuum caufis, siue de Incantationibus*. Basileae: Cum caef. Maieftatis gratia & priuilegio, 1656

Pomponazzi, Pietro. *Les Causes des Merveilles de la Nature ou Les Enchantements*, tr. Henri Busson. Paris: *Les Éditions Rieder*, 1930

Porres, Antonio Montes de. *Syma de D. Antonio Diana*. Madrid: Melchor Sanchez, 1657

Porta, Io. Baptista. *Magiae Natvralis, sive De Miracvlis Rervm Natvralivm Antverpiae: In aedibus Ioannis Steelfij*, 1562

Portae, Io. Bapt. *Magiae Natvralis*. Neapoli: *Apud Horatium Saluianum*, 1589

Porta, Jean Baptiste. *La Magie Naturelle*. Roven: Chez Jacques Lucas, 1680

Porta, John Baptista. Natural Magick, Anonymous, tr. London: Printed for Thomas Young, and Samuel Speed, 1658

Proust, Marcel. *Du Coté de Chez Swann*. Paris: Gaston Gallimard, 1919

Real Academia Española, dle.rae.es

Redi, Francesco. Bacchus in Tuscany, tr. Leigh Hunt. London: Printed for John and H. L. Hunt, 1825

---------------------- *Bacco in Toscana*. Firenze: Per Piero Matini, 1685

Remigii, Nicolai. *Daemonolatreiae Libri Tres*. Coloniae: Apud Henricum Falckenburg, 1596

Remy, Nicolas. <u>Demonolatry</u>, tr. E. A. Ashwin, ed. Montague Summers. London: John Rodker, 1930

Ristori, R. <u>Biographical Dictionary of the Italians</u>, treccani.it

Robinette, Glenn. <u>Did Lin Zexu Make Morphine?</u> vols. II, III. Valparaiso, Chile: Graffiti Militante Press, 2008, 2020

Rojas, Ioanne a. *De fuccefsioniibus, De Haereticis, et Singularia in fidei fauorem*. *Salamanticae: Ex officina Ildefonfi à. Terranoua & Neyla*, 1581

Rojas Zorrilla, Francisco de. *Lo que queria ver el Marqués de Villena*, fouind in *Biblioteca de Autores Españoles, Comedias Escogidas*, ed. Ramón de Mesonero Romanos. Madrid: Imprenta de Hernando y Compania, 1897

Ronsard, Pierre de. *Oeuvres Completes de P. de Ronsard*, vol. 8, ed. Paul Laumonier. Paris: Librarie Alphonse Lemerre, 1919

Rosenthal, R. J. and Faris, Suzanne. "The etymology and early history of 'addiction,'" *Addiction Research and Theory*, 27 (2), February 2019

Roth, Cecil. <u>A History of the Marranos</u>, fourth edition. NY: Schocken Books, 1974

--------------- <u>The Spanish Inquisition</u>. New York: W. W. Norton & Company, 1964

Rousseau, Abbé. *Secrets et Remedes Eprovez*, second edition. Paris: Chez Claude Jombert, 1718

Ruiz de Alarcón, Hernando. *Tratado de las supersticiones y costumbres gentilicas que hoy viven entre los indios naturales de esta Nueva España*. Mexico, D. F.: Fuente Cultural, 1953

----------------------------------- Treatise on the Heathen Surperstitions, tr. J. Richard Andrews and Ross Hassig. Norman, OK: University of Oklahoma Press, 1984

Ruiz de Montoya, Antonio. The Spiritual Conquest, tr. C. J. McNaspy et al. St. Louis, MO: The Institute of Jesuit Sources, 1993 (1639)

-------------------------------- *Conquista Espiritval*. Madrid: En la imprenta del Reyno, 1639

Sachs, Hans. *Eygentlich Befchreibung Aller Stande Auff Erden*. Franckfurt am Mayn: Feyerbents, 1568

Saint-Sauver, Jacques Grasset de. *Encyclopédie des Voyages: Asie*. Paris: Chez Deroy, 1796

Sala, Angelo. *Opiologia*. La Haye, NL: Chez Hillebrant Iacobffz, 1614

Scot, Reginald. The Difcouerie of Witchcraft. London: By Henry Davidson for William Brome, 1584

Serrano y Sanz, M. *Autobiografías y Memorías*. Madrid: Librería Editorial de Bailly/Balliére é Hijos, 1905

Sévigné, Marie de Rabutin-Chantal, marquise de. Letters of Madame de Sévigné, vols. IV, V, VII, IX. London: Printed for J. Walker et al., 1811

-- *Lettres de Madame de Sévigné*, Tomes III, VI. Paris: Librarie de L. Hachette et Cie, 1863

-- *Recueil Des Lettres de Madame de Sévigné*, Tome Huitième. A Avignon: Chez Fr. Chambeau, 1804

Sigerist, Henry E. Paracelsus in the Light of Four Hundred Years. NY: Columbia University Press, 1941

---------------------- "Laudanum in the Works of Paracelsus," *Bulletin of the History of Medicine*, vol. 9, no. 5 (May 1941), Johns Hopkins University Press

Simancas, Diego de. *De catholicis institutionibus*. Romae: In Aedibus Populi Romani, 1575

Solis, Antonio de. The History of the Conquest of Mexico by the Spaniards, vol. I, tr. Thomas Townsend, ed. Nathaniel Hooke. London: Printed for John Osborn, 1738

Sprenger, R. P. F. Iacobo. *Malleus Maleficarum, in Tres divisus Partes*. *Venetiis : Ad candentis Salamandrae infigne*, 1574

Stella, Benedetto. *Il Tabacco Opera*. Roma: Per Filippo Maria Mancini, 1669

Stephen, Leslie, ed. Dictionary of National Biography, vol. XXL, Garnet – Gloucester. NY: MacMillan and Co., 1890

Stoddart, Anna M. The Life of Paracelsus. London: John Murray, 1911

Strachey, William. The Historie of Travaile into Virginia Britannia, ed. R. H. Major. London: Printed for the Hakylut Society, 1849

Summers, Montague. The Discovery of Witches: A Study of Master Matthew Hopkins. London: At the Cayne Press, 1928

------------------------- tr. The Malleus Maleficarum of Heinrich Kramer and James Sprenger. London: John Rodker, 1928

Sydenham, Thomas. The Entire Works of Dr Thomas Sydenham, tr. John Swain. London: Printed by R. Cave, 1763

------------------------- The Works of Thomas Sydenham, M. D. on Acute and Chronic Diseases, ed. Benjamin Rush. Philadelphia: E. Kimber et al, 1815

Tedeschi, John. "Literary Piracy in Seventeenth-Century Florence: Giovanni Battista Neri's '*De iudice S. inquisitionis opusculum*,'" *Huntington Library Quarterly*, vol. 50, no. 2 (Spring, 1987)

BIBLIOGRAPHY

Ugarte, Rubén Vargas, ed. _Concilios Limenses (1551 – 1772)_, vol. I. Lima: Imprimatur Juan, Cardenal Guevara, 1951

Ukers, William H. All About Coffee. NY: The Tea and Coffee Trade Journal Company, 1922

Unknown. The Diary of Christopher Columbus, Research at King's College London, Early Modern Spain, Diary of 1492, ems.kcl.ac.uk

Unknown. _Escritvras, Acverdos, Administraciones, y Svplicas_. Madrid: Por Diego Diaz de la Carrera, 1659

Unknown. "The Narcotics we indulge in – Part II," _Blackwood's Edinburgh Magazine_, vol. LSSIV, July-Dec 1853 (American edition, vol. XXXVII). NY: Leonard Scot and Company, 1853

Valencia, Pedro de. _Pedro de Valencia: Obras Completas_, eds. Manuel Antonio Marcos Casquero é Hipólito B. Riesco Álvarez, vol. VII. _León: Secretariado de Publicaciones de la Universidad de León_, 1997

Vámbéry, Ármin. Travels in Central Asia. NY: Harper & Brothers, 1865

---------------------- History of Bokhara, 2nd ed. London: Henry S. King & Co., 1873

Van Dyke, C. and Byck, R. _"Cocaína," Investigación y Ciencia_, 68, 1982

Varenne, G. _El abuso de las drogas_. Madrid: Guadarrama, 1973

Vargas Machuca, Bernardo de. _Milicia y Descripción de las Indias_, vol. I. Madrid: Librería de Victoriano Suarez, 1892 (1599)

Vetancurt, Augustín de. _Teatro Mexicano_, Tom. I. En Mexico: por Doña Maria de Benavides Viuda de Iuan de Ribera, 1698

Virchow, Rudolf. _Ueber Nahrungs- und Genussmittel_. Berlin: C. G. Lüderitz'sche Verlagsbuchhandlung, 1868

Waite, Arthur Edward, ed. The Hermetic and Alchemical Writings of Aureolus Philippus Theophrastus Bambast, of Hohenheim, called Paracelsus the Great, vol. II. London: James Elliott and Co., 1894

Wecker, John et al. Eighteen Books of the Secrets of Art & Nature. London: Simon Miller, 1660

Wier, Iean. Histoires Dispvtes et Discovrs: Des Illvsions et impostvres des diables, des magiciens infames, sorcieres et empoisonnevrs, tr. Iaques Grevin, vol. I. Paris: Aux Bureaux du Progrès Médical/A. Delahaye et Lecrosnier, 1885

Wieri, Ioannis. Opera Omnia. Amstelodami: Apud Petrum Vanden Berge, 1660

Willis, Thomas. Pharmaceutice Rationalis: or, an Exercitation of the Operations of Medicine in Humane Bodies, Part One. London: Printed for T. Dring, C. Harper, and F. Leigh, 1679

-------------------- Pharmaceutice Rationalis sive Diatriba de Medicamentorum Operationibus in Humano Corpore, third edition. Oxoniae: E. Theatro Sheldoniano, 1679

World Health Organization, Internationally Peer Reviewed Chemical Safety Information, Inchem.org

Zalta, Edward N., ed. Stanford Encyclopaedia of Philosophy, plato.stanford.edu

Index
Volume Two Part Two

INDEX

INDEX

INDEX

INDEX

www.ingramcontent.com/pod-product-compliance
Lightning Source LLC
Chambersburg PA
CBHW030415100426
42812CB00028B/2977/J